Murder & Mystery in the Highlands

BY THE SAME AUTHOR

The Highlands and Islands
(*The Regions of Britain Series*)

The Supernatural Highlands

Murder & Mystery in the Highlands

Francis Thompson

LONDON
ROBERT HALE LIMITED

© *Francis Thompson 1977*

First published in Great Britain 1977

ISBN 0 7091 6370 3

Robert Hale Limited
Clerkenwell House
Clerkenwell Green
London EC1R 0HT

PRINTED IN GREAT BRITAIN BY
CLARKE, DOBLE & BRENDON LTD,
PLYMOUTH AND LONDON

Contents

Illustrations

PICTURE CREDITS

Hamish Campbell: 1–5, 8, 9, 12–24, 26–28; J. W. Macrae: 6, 7, 10, 11; National Maritime Museum: 25

Introduction

On the morning of the 13th September 1803, William Wordsworth and his sister Dorothy trudged their way over the hills from Loch Katrine to go down Loch Voil. They passed some deserted mountain huts, upon which they reflected and, on a green mound outside one of them, William "conceived the notion of writing an ode upon the affecting subject of those relics of human society found in that grand and solitary region". The two travellers were in a meditative mood as they descended into the strath, the scene before them being one which deepened their feeling of gentle melancholy. Dorothy wrote in her Journal: "It was harvest-time, and the fields were quietly—might I be allowed to say pensively?—enlivened by small companies of reapers". Recollection of the scene later prompted her to copy out William's poem "The Solitary Reaper", which itself was suggested by a sentence in Thomas Wilkinson's *Tour in Scotland*:

Will no one tell me what she sings?
Perhaps the plaintive numbers flow
For old, unhappy, far-off things,
And battles long ago:
Or is it some more humble lay,
Familiar matter of today?
Some natural sorrow, loss, or pain,
That has been, and may be again?

Wordsworth caught the whole essence of living in the Highlands; far from being a pleasant idyllic living, it was harsh, forbidding and unrelenting; and it demanded from the people who wrested a living from both land and the sea a certain high degree of commitment to live a life which stifled any thought and action for the possible creation of a lifestyle which could enhance the physical conditions which surrounded them, nor, to a lesser extent, the creation of a mental environment in which their minds could expand to gain greater spiritual satisfaction. Rather the land was a hard master, demanding all their waking time to make it yield produce enough to keep body and soul together, to see one year begin anew and hope to see it end as well. But this was not all. The uncertainty of life itself added a particular and peculiar edge to living in the region, where one day might see the sunrise over the hills, swathing the glens with its light, and the setting of the same sun might yet be seen through eyes dimmed by impending death as one's lifeblood spilled slowly onto the ground: the result of a raid, sudden and swift, by a neighbouring clan seeking revenge for a wrong, real or imagined, done many generations before.

Today the Highland region is still seen in the same kind of romantic haze as it was in Wordsworth's day. Thomas Campbell's statement that "distance lends enchantment to the view" was true in the context of the Scottish Highlands and Islands and they have suffered as the result, being placed in a scenic framework to inspire the noble thought, rather than being viewed as a region with a thick red line of tragedy running sinister across its face. Many travellers, particularly in the eighteenth and nineteenth centuries, picked up snatches of past history and committed them to the printed page, so that readers were able to appreciate the harshness of life and living which could be put down to something other than aboriginals eking out an existence in an unrelated kaleidoscope of poverty and wretchedness.

Volumes have been written on the clan system which held sway in the Highlands and Islands for many centuries. Indeed, there are few instances more remarkable in the political history of any country than the succession of Highland chiefs and the long and uninterrupted control which they had over their territories and their followers. Clans held together by recognizing a common name or identifying with a certain territory. Within the clan, and particularly in the formative years, there were many close relationships, by blood and fosterage, which all helped to make the clan something more than a tribe with an imposed or elected hierarchy. Consequently, there was ever present a fierce loyalty to the clan head, a loyalty which was seen both in its most admirable and its most pitiful aspects when external political forces invaded the hereditary rights of the clan chief to pressurize him into looking to the south rather than to his chief's duties to his followers. Particularly during the long era of the Highland Clearances, clansmen could hardly begin to understand their chiefs' changing attitudes to their relationship with him, and the land, which had never been called into question. Almost overnight, clansmen, who had thought 'themselves to have an inalienable right to the land, found themselves on one side, usually the losing side, of a new and bewildering legal relationship, in which the chief consolidated his position by title deeds. Not all clan chiefs, however, resorted to clearing their former clansmen off the land; but too many did so and by their action alienated themselves from clan tradition. However, long before the cracks began to show, loyalty to the clan chief was almost a qualitative element in life, upholding the right and power of life and death of the chief over the clan. So fierce was the loyalty it gave second place to the authority of the king whose mandates could neither stop the depredations of one clan against another, nor allay their mutual hostilities. The clan system, by repudiating the authority of the sovereign, who often, in any case, showed himself to be little concerned with the realities and intangibles which held a clan together, and of his laws, prevented clans from ever coming to any general terms of accommodation for settling their differences. The consequence was that their feuds were interminable, their quarrels endless and their country was for centuries the theatre of petty warfare and bloodshed. Against the position of the chief, held in such esteem, any king had a hard task of it to act as intermediary to gain peaceful settlement for the good of all and, in particular, the common folk of the Highlands who could rarely guarantee that they would see the dawn of the following day, or if they did, the dusk of the same day, except perhaps through bloody tears and despair. The cold service which kings were often able to buy, could rarely match the hot enthusiasm for any endeavour on which a chief had pronounced.

The roots of many centuries-old clan feuds often began in insult, or some personal affront to the chief and so to his followers.

Often feuds were carried over the succeeding generations until only legend carried a mere grain of truth as to their origins. Other reasons for feuding included the illegal annexation of territory, or the winning of territory by forced marriage. Inevitably, some clans took advantage of the unsettled state of each era and consolidated themselves into positions of importance, as often as not allying themselves to the royal personage of the day, and so achieving the means for the aggrandizement of themselves and the clan. These tactics, however, produced suspicion and enmity which in later centuries could still arouse fear. One thinks of MacIan of Glencoe being genuinely troubled at having to go to Inveraray to see the Sheriff to swear fealty to King William, knowing that the place was swarming with his unsympathetic and traditional enemies. Similarly James Stewart of the Glen feared the outcome of his trial, overriden as it was with Campbells.

Highland history is crammed full with incidents in which blood was shed for one reason or another. Indeed, there is hardly a district or locality in the Highlands and Islands which has not been the scene of some bloody feudal encounter. The list of antagonists is almost endless with an unbelievable number of permutations: Munroes and Clan Chattan; Clan Chattan and the MacKays; Clan Chattan and the Camerons; The MacKays and the Rosses; Mac-Donalds against the MacKenzies, the MacKays, the MacLeans, the MacDougalls, the Camerons, the Campbells, the Frasers, the Gunns, and even different septs of the MacLeods. The very names of MacDonald of Sleat, Clanranald, Glengarry, Keppoch and Glencoe indicate battles and bloodshedding and pepper the pages of Highland history. Treachery and double-dealing abounded. The Macgregors and the Colquhouns fought a desperate battle in Glenfruin in 1603, when the latter were routed with the loss of 200 men. So very indignant was Colquhoun, Laird of Luss, that he misrepresented the whole affair to King James VI, before the latter quitted Scotland for London, with a great display of 200 bloody shirts from the bodies of his slain vassals to indicate to the King the cruelty of the Macgregors. His Majesty, without hearing both sides, grew incensed at the Macgregors and proclaimed them rebels and interdicted all his lieges in Scotland from harbouring a single soul of them. Heavy fines were imposed on all who sheltered any of the unfortunate clan. The fines were punctually levied and as punctually pocketed by the Earl of Argyll as recompense for his services against the maligned and persecuted Clan Macgregor.

If the search for revenge for wrongs had been undertaken by individual champions of the clan chiefs, then perhaps many innocents might have escaped some of the dreadful fates which they met. Innocently worshipping in church, they could die from fire and suffocation. Others, going about their everyday business of herding or farming, could find themselves the target of armed men with waving swords rushing over the top of a nearby hill. Yet others could be imprisoned unjustly for years, or else got rid of by being fed salt beef with no water to slake the ensuing thirst. Often some ingenuity was exercised in making an insult. One instance occurred in 1601 when Domhnall Gorm Mor of Sleat in Skye married Margaret, sister of Sir Roderick MacLeod, commonly called Rory Mor of Dunvegan. But, for some "displeasure of jealousy conceived against her", Domhnall Gorm sent his wife back to her brother. This was insult enough, but it was compounded. The lady concerned had the misfortune to be blind of an eye and to show all the indignity in his power, her erstwhile husband procured a one-eyed horse for her, a one-eyed valet, and a one-eyed terrier. When the single-sighted party arrived at last at Dunvegan, Rory Mor hardly needed the sight of his own two good eyes to see the insult given to him by the chief of the MacDonalds. Revenge was needed and the avenging forces met at the base of the Cuillin Hills, where the fierce fighting went on with terrible slaughter.

Of course, clansmen ventured outside their own territory for reasons other than those of honest trade and feuding. Clan wars, or at least sporadic skirmishes between clans, were at one time an accepted part of life. Many incidents were connected with what was euphemistically called 'cattle-lifting'. In wild and thinly-inhabited country, full of places to hide for long periods without detection, there was an obvious temptation to drive away someone else's cattle roaming in the hills. By the middle of the eighteenth century, however, those who took part in such expeditions seem generally to have been 'broken men', who belonged to no particular clan and were possibly regarded simply as outlaws. They operated particularly successfully near the lowlands, where there was less danger of retaliation. Rannoch, for example, was "in an uncivilized barbarous state, under no check, or restraint of laws" prior to 1745. Gangs from Rannoch, according to the *Old Statistical Account for Scotland*, ". . . laid the whole country, from Stirling to Coupar of Angus, under contribution, obliging the inhabitants to pay them Black Meal, as it is called, to save their property from being plundered. This was the centre of this kind of traffic. In the months of September and October they gathered to the number of about 300, built temporary huts, drank whisky all the time, settled accounts for stolen cattle, and received balances. It would have required a regiment to have a thief brought from that country. . . . The victims tried to protect themselves by organizing armed bands to fight off the raiders; but the honesty of these in turn came into question, and it was alleged that they sometimes used their position to travel about the country under the pretence of enquiring after stolen cattle, but actually preparing for depredations of their own. Suspicion, conflict and occasional warfare were thus the order of the Day."

Scant regard for the law became an inborn thing. Even in the early decades of the nineteenth century, travellers such as Coleridge and Southey sensed and recorded that the Highlands were conscious of the great injustices done to them and their forebears, particularly by non-Highlanders. At an inn in Glencoe Southey "observed these names written with a pencil on the window shutter, Henri de Ravaillac and Pierre Marat. It is worthy of notice, as showing what kind of spirits are abroad". Coleridge was "taken for a spy and clapped into Fort Augustus", an incident which indicated that fifty-eight years after Culloden the authorities in the Highlands suffered from a nervous political twitch and displayed considerable jumpiness. It has been suggested that while there was undoubtedly an undercurrent of insurrection running through the Highlands, there was no real attempt or even desire to foment actual revolution. The clans had been too broken at Culloden to try. Indeed, when the people of Ross-shire initially rose against the introduction into their midst of the Cheviot sheep, in a movement which was innocent of any intention other than driving out the sheep, they were immediately labelled as a dangerous and seditious mob. It was to the practical advantage of the lairds to see in the Highlanders what John Prebble (in his book *The Highland Clearances*) calls "the chimera of these days, a monster in a red cap waving hands of blood". Whether they did this out of vanity for a heroic role or out of a machiavellian desire to exaggerate a threat, the better to gather a national force to crush it, is irrelevant, since the outcome was the terrible injustice heaped on the heads of the people. There was no doubt, too, that the authorities in the Highlands, in particular, out of all Britain, were nervous that the flash point in social aspirations provided by the French Revolution, and still dangerously near lighting point well into the nineteenth century, would blow up in their faces —for the urban and rural poor were ever regarded as being potential revolutionaries having, to some degree, assimilated Republican tendencies. Many of those in authority feared that the traditional laws and institutions of the country would fall before a policy derived from fear and mistaken expedience. There were, in fact, doomed attempts at insurrection at Peterloo and, in 1819, at the 'Battle of Bonnymuir'. With such an atmosphere in the country, and with their past history counting against them, the Highlanders were more feared than most when it came to potential insurrection.

Travellers in the Highland region in the eighteenth and nineteenth centuries noted an acceptance of diminished responsibility to laws created and enacted in some faraway place such as Edinburgh and, even farther, London. They recorded their impressions, as did Edwart Burt:

> High-bridge, a fine bridge of three arches flung across the torrent Spean, founded on rocks; two of the three arches are ninety-five feet high. This bridge was built by General Wade, in order to form a communication with the country. These publick works were at first very disagreeable to the old Chieftains, and lessened their influence greatly; for by admitting strangers among them, their clans were taught that the Lairds were not the first of men. But they had another reason much more solid: Lochaber had been a den

of thieves; and as long as they had their waters, their torrents and their bogs, in a state of nature, they made their excursions, could plunder and retreat with their booty in full security. So weak were the laws in many parts of North Britain, till after the late rebellion, that no stop could be put to this infamous practice. A contribution, called the Black-meal, was raised by several of these plundering chieftains over a vast extent of country—whoever payd it had their cattle ensured, but those who dared to refuse were sure to suffer. Many of these freebooters were wont to insert an article, by which they were to be released from their agreement, in case of any civil commotion: thus, at the breaking out of the last rebellion, a M'Gregor, who had with the strictest honor (till that event) preserved his friends' cattle, immediately sent them word, that from that time they were out of his protection, and must now take care of themselves. Barrisdale was another of this class, chief of a band of robbers who spread terror over the whole country: but the Highlanders at that time esteemed the open theft of cattle, or the making of a creach (as they call it), by no means dishonorable; and the young men considered it a piece of gallantry, by which they recommended themselves to their mistresses. On the other side there was often as much bravery in the pursuers; for frequent battles ensued, and much blood has been spilt on these occasions. They also shewed great dexterity in tracing the robbers, not only through the boggy land, but over the firmest ground, and even over places where other cattle had passed, knowing well how to distinguish the steps of those that were wandering about from those that were driven hastily away by the Free-booters.

Thomas Pennant, another noted and often-quoted Highland traveller recorded:

There is not an instance of any country having made so sudden a change in its morals as this I have just visited, and the vast tract intervening between these coasts and Loch-Ness. Security and civilisation possesses every part; yet thirty years have not elapsed since the whole was a den of thieves, of the most extraordinary kind. They conducted their plundering excursions with the utmost policy, and reduced the whole art of theft into a regular system. From habit it lost all the appearance of criminalty: they considered it as laboring in their vocation; and when a party was formed for any expedition against their neighbour's property, they and their friends prayed as earnestly to heaven for success, as if they were engaged in the most laudable design. . . .

The greatest robbers were used to preserve hospitality to those that came to their houses, and, like the wild Arabs, observed the strictest honor towards their guests, or those that put implicit confidence in them. The Kennedies, two common thieves, took the Young Pretender under protection, and kept him with faith inviolate, notwithstanding they knew an immense reward was offered for his head. They often robbed for his support, and to supply him with linen they once surprized the baggage horses of one of our general officers. They often went in disguise to Inverness to buy provisions for him. At length, a very considerable time after, one of these poor fellows, who had virtue to resist the temptation of thirty thousand pounds, was hanged for stealing a cow, value thirty shillings.

The greatest crime among these felons was that of infidelity among themselves: the criminal underwent a summary trial, and, if convicted, never missed of a capital punishment. . . . When one man had a claim on another, but wanted power to make it good, it was held lawful for him to steal from his debtor as many cattle as would satisfy his demand, provided he sent notice (as soon as he got out of reach of pursuit) that he had them, and would return them, provided satisfaction was made on a certain day agreed on. When a creach or great expedition had been made against distant herds, the owners, as soon as discovery was made, rose in arms, and with all their friends made instant pursuit, tracing the cattle by their track for perhaps scores of miles. Their nicety in distinguishing that of their cattle from those that were only casually wandering, or driven, was amazingly sagacious. As soon as they arrived on an estate where the track was lost, they immediately attacked the proprietor, and would oblige him to recover the track from his land forwards, or to make good the loss they had sustained. This custom had the force of law, which gave to the Highlanders this surprising skill in the art of tracking. It has been observed before, that to steal, rob and plunder with dexterity, was esteemed as the highest act of heroism. The feuds between the great families was one great cause. There was not a chieftain but that kept, in some remote valley in the depth of wood and rocks, whole tribes of thieves in readiness to let loose against his neighbours; when, from some public or private reason, he did not judge it expedient to resent openly any real or imaginary affront. From this motive the greater chieftain-robbers always supported the lesser, and encouraged no sort of improvement on their estates but what promoted rapine.

In decades nearer to present times, Highlanders in British regiments and on land, sea and in the air have figured largely in both

world wars of this century and in the many wars of the nineteenth century. Indeed, some measure of the contribution of some
areas in the Highlands is instanced by Scotland's war losses—all
perhaps stemming from an attitude of mind in the seat of government in far-off London, as stated by General Wolfe who, in advo-
cating the employment of Highlanders in British military service,
wrote: "I should imagine that Highlanders might be of use.
They are hardy, intrepid, accustomed to a rough country, and no
great mischief if they fall. How can you better employ a secret
enemy than by making his end conducive to the common good? If
this sentiment should take wind what an execrable and bloody
being should I be considered." In the 1914–18 war, Scotland's
losses were in the neighbourhood of 110,000 and possibly more.
The total loss suffered by the United States from a population
then of about twenty-five times that of Scotland was 126,000.
The island of Lewis lost 1,151 men out of 6,712 men serving in
the forces, something in the region of seventeen per cent. Some
Highland villages lost one man out of every three.

This book may shatter the romantic image many have of the
region, an image which has been carefully cultured by those
agencies wholly concerned with the promotion of the region as an
immediately-accessible and easily-assimilated scenic environment,
a breathing space from industrialized urbanity, in which the people,
'the aboriginals', have little or no place (probably because by and
large in the tourist-oriented scheme of things, they have little or
no say in the manner in which the region is presented to visitors).
But it is as well to remember that all tracts of land have their
histories, both good and bad, which have involved the people of the
past. While this book might dwell, for the sake of encompassing
the subject of its title, on the deterioration of human relationships
and the failure to establish trustworthy links of communication between communities or clans of differing origins, with consequences
which involved the shedding of blood, we should not look at the
old Highland society in isolation but against the background of
other societies, with equally demanding norms of honour to be
satisfied and which led to blood-letting on comparable scales. In

general, human society being what it is, an intellectual but un-
thinking animal, unable to cope with the basic needs of friendship and mutual understanding, it was no different in other parts
of the world than in the Highlands of Scotland, and so one might,
with some small effort at credibility, still retain the age-old image
of a people whose character was inherently as wild as was their
mountainous and harsh environment, both natural and man-made.

While the book takes the reader into the recent past, with some
mysteries and murders, it might be useful to point out that according to the latest statistics, less crime is committed per 1,000 head
of the population in the Highlands and Islands of Scotland than
in any other part of Great Britain. Where there has been a notice-
able increase involving police activity of one kind or another, leading to prosecution in court, this has invariably been due to the
influence of incoming populations from other parts of the country,
following work opportunities, and bringing in different values
which reflect the social backgrounds of their previous communities.

ONE

Legendary Precedents

It is something of a paradox that the Highlands and Islands, now so much associated with romance, duly leavened with heavy bastings of Celtic twilight, have also produced some of the best military resources in the British Isles. The martial qualities of the Highlander have been noted both by historians and by practical and shrewd politicians who forever looked to the north of Scotland for men to form the regiments which kept the four corners of the erstwhile British Empire together with tooth and nail in the eighteenth and nineteenth centuries. Thus, there are many precedents for that side of the Highland character which displays a down-to-earth disregard for danger and revels in acts of bravery. But when these characteristics are sparked off by other elements, such as a fierce and unrelenting pride in clan, name and land, with the need to save honour above life, it comes as no surprise to find that twists in the alchemy have produced men who have committed acts which are often so much out of the normal context.

But these men have precedents going back some two millennia and more: back to the origins of Scotland, in Ireland, where the early beginnings of Celt and Gael took place. Caesar and other writers have written about the habits and manners of the nations the Romans fought, including the Celtae or Celts of Gaul, a region which included both the France and the Switzerland of the present day. From time to time this race crossed over the Channel into Britain, in two distinct streams: the Gaels (Gaedhils or Goidels) and the Britons or Brythons. The former are to be found in Ireland, in Mannin, and in the northern and western parts of Scotland. The latter are found in Cornwall, Wales and Brittany. With a characteristic disregard for the written word, the traditions, lore, laws and customs of the Celts were carefully stored away in the computer-like minds of the early Druids; transmission of information from one generation to another was by oral means using techniques which have lasted to the present day as efficient and reliable methods of cultural transmission. Among these traditions were stories of the old warriors of the race, locked away in the mists of antiquity that, if early writers are to be believed, started about the year 2242 in the 'Age of the World', some forty days before the Flood.

Some two thousand years ago the Irish were engaged in foreign activities in an endeavour to extend their territories, particularly in Alba (Scotland), Britain and the west of France. Their young chiefs seem to have been sent to Scotland to study the arts of both peace and war, and the friendly communications which eventually obtained between the two countries points to the existence of Gaelic-speaking settlements on the western coasts of Scotland. This colonizing brought into Scotland the traditions of the Irish. Slowly the settings for the brave deeds of heroes were given a Scottish locale; warriors like Fionn, Cuchullin and others became a common possession and their stories were told around firesides in both Alba and in Erin. Some Highland clans even began to trace their origins to Irish bravadoes such as Conn of the Hundred Battles to claim them among their ancestors.

However, it is possible to winnow some particularly Scottish elements from the large and significant corpus of Irish tales and some of these follow. Perforce they must be short versions of the originals, for some classic tales take many hours—and some even days—in their telling. The people of the Scottish Highlands have tended to retain more of the tales of the Fionn cycle while in Ireland tales of the Cuchullin cycle have been better preserved.

The magically-controlled tales about Fionn Mac Cumhail and his Fiana have been popular with all generations of Highlanders who marvelled at the exploits. This may be because Fionn's exploits were more associated with the common folk of the land than with the ruling classes. By the sixteenth century Fionn was a more prominent figure in every stratum of Gaelic narrative lore than many of the previous heroes and gods, such as Lugh, Cuchullin,

Conaire and those other characters who, by their rank, held the prominent places in the words of the storytellers. By the early eighteenth century, Fionn, under the new name of Fingal, became a household word wherever the romantic literary movement had taken root. For this we have to thank the Scot James Macpherson who, in 1762 and 1763, published his *Fingal* and *Temora*, supposed to have been translated from epic poems written by 'Ossian' in the third and fourth centuries of our era. However, the epics were largely a figment of Macpherson's imagination; even so, the names of the heroes, and some of the incidents described, were based on genuine Gaelic balladry about Fionn, Ossian, Oscar, and other members of the Fiana. Men such as Napoleon and Goethe loved to read Macpherson's work, which was translated into many languages and helped to awaken the interest in Celtic studies which has resulted in proving that Macpherson was nothing more than a translator, but even that, as a benefit, has established Celtic tradition as one of very long standing and, indeed, one of the important contributory streams of European literature.

Among the ancient Celtic heroes was Diarmad. One of the Fingalians, he was the bravest in battle. His mother was the only sister of Fionn, who ever looms large in the old traditional long-tales of the Gaelic-speaking Highlands. Whatever prowess Diarmad had on the field of battle, he had similar successes with women. One in particular, Grainne, the wife of Fionn, fell for him one day as she was walking along the shore in Skye and met him returning after a successful hunt. After greeting him she placed on him the three spells of love, lest he should remain unaware of her passion for him. Diarmad was certainly affected by the beautiful Grainne and they both resolved to leave the place, to make for the hills and lonely mountain tracks so that Fionn and his followers, when they discovered the elopement, would not be able to catch them.

The couple journeyed through the woods for a long time until they reached a quiet and attractive spot to refresh themselves. Glad to have some respite they settled down for the night. But, before dawn, they were woken up by the yelling of hounds. Ill luck had brought Fionn and his men to the very place chasing after a poison-boar. Chance now brought the two men face to face;

Diarmad was suddenly ashamed at his deed, Grainne's love charms now having worn off a bit. Fionn, however, did not show offence. Instead, he invited Diarmad to join in the boar hunt. It took a whole day to track the beast down, to be killed by Diarmad. Great was the rejoicing of Fionn and the people of the district who had for long been terrorized by the fierce animal.

But then a dispute arose between Fionn and Diarmad about the length of the boar. Diarmad, in an attempt to measure the animal, suffered a finger pierced by a poison bristle. In intense pain, Diarmad pleaded with Fionn to go to Tobar an Eun, the Well of the Birds, to fill his cupped hands with some of the healing water. Fionn went willingly to the well, but on his way back he thought of how Diarmad had attempted to steal his wife Grainne and, in a growing rage, dashed the water from his hands to the ground. Diarmad, after all, had committed an act against their friendship and so should pay the fullest penalty in consequence. Remorse, however, overtook Fionn and he hurried back to the well again for more water. But by the time he reached Diarmad, the latter had died. And, while Diarmad was being buried, Grainne, stricken with grief, leaped into the closing grave to lie with her dead lover. Other districts in the Highlands, and in Ireland, claim credit for the fight between the boar and Diarmad, including Glenelg, Lorne, Kintyre and Perthshire.

Cuchullin appears in both Irish and Scottish cycles of mythological tales. In the Irish cycle, the "Tarn of Cuchullin", he is a great hero, larger than life, a young warrior enjoying his spectacular strength with no thought beyond fighting and being fêted of all men. He often used magic, and, indeed was only half of the physical world; his feet were firmly fixed in the strange otherworld of the Celt. He had merely to enter a battle to be victorious, or to look at a woman to win her over into his arms. In the Ossian stories, in the Scottish cycle, Cuchullin is a man torn for love between his wife and his duty to the child king of Ulster, whose guardian he is. Duty wins the day and Fate decrees that he be defeated and killed in saving Ulster. But his heart remained always in Dunscaith, his island of Skye home.

In James Macpherson's *Ossian*, it is at Dunscaith that Cuchullin landed when he first came to Skye; Skye, indeed, was the home and love of his manhood. In the *Ossian* story, Cuchullin and his heroes build Dunscaith in a single night. He was always happy there until word came that the King of Lochlainn (Scandinavia) was on his way to attack Ulster, whose king was the child Cormac, Cuchullin's ward. Landing in Ulster, to save the province, Cuchullin's men were outnumbered and though they fought bravely from dawn to dusk, the battle went on without any decisive victory.

On the following day another great battle was fought, ending in the defeat of Cuchullin. The third day, rallying his men, Cuchullin held off the Scandinavians until help arrived in the shape of Fingal and the rest of the Ulster chiefs. Utterly defeated now, Cuchullin handed his sword to Fingal, as one no longer fit to wear it. However, his efforts had saved Ulster. Fingal returned the sword and persuaded Cuchullin to return to Dunscaith, with due rewards. But Cuchullin had foreseen his own death and stayed on to fight; during the following day he was killed. And, as Dunscaith had been built in a single night, so it fell back into ruins after Cuchullin's wife, Bragelam, died of a broken heart.

Many centuries later, when Dunscaith was in the hands of the MacDonalds of Sleat, after wresting it from the Clan MacLeod—which deed was one of the many which provided numberless grounds for feuding between the two clans—one of the MacDonald chiefs made peace with his neighbour and gave a daughter in marriage to one of MacLeod's sons. But the girl had other views and opposed the marriage furiously, for she had not been consulted; however, in due time the marriage did take place. But that was not the end of the matter. Later the reluctant wife bore two sons. But her hatred for her husband and his family remained unabated. One day the whole family returned to Dunscaith for a visit, MacDonald being it was believed, very devoted to the two boys, his only grandchildren. He and young MacLeod went out hunting. On their return they were met, much to their surprise by a smiling wife who told them to hurry as she herself had prepared such a savoury fawn as they had never tasted. Hungrily they ate well and praised her cooking. Then she said, shouting, 'Now you know my devotion. I have cooked my children for your dinner and you have eaten them! No heirs for MacLeod!' And she threw herself from the window onto the rocks below.

Yet another of the many incidents recorded by tradition about Dunscaith concerned Donald Gruamach (the Grim) who married a Clanranald woman and lived in the castle. Once, while his wife was entertaining twelve of her kinsmen, a cousin of Donald's, Ranald MacDonald from North Uist, who had an ongoing feud with her kinsmen, arrived to visit. Highland hospitality being at its traditional best in a chief's house, Ranald was made welcome. He stayed the night and very early next morning rose to make his departure. Donald Gruamach was full of protest at the early departure and finally remarked, "At least stay to say farewell to my wife". "If I stay she will not thank me," replied Ranald who hurried away at great speed. In due course, Donald's wife rose and went to the window to see, not the sunrise, but twelve corpses of her kinsmen, killed by Ranald. Indeed, she was not pleased and eventually made successful plans to have Ranald assassinated for his work on that particular night.

One Highland clan which traces its origins deep in Irish history is the MacNeils of Barra. The clan claims its descent from Niall Naoighiallach, known as Neil of the Nine Hostages, who, on the decease of King Crimthann, became High-King of Ireland in A.D. 379 and reigned at Tara until A.D. 405. Neil's mother was Carthan of the Black Locks, taken captive by Eochaidh, his father, who already had several sons by his queen. Apprehensive lest, on the death of Eochaidh, the eldest son of a woman in bondage should deprive her own firstborn of his birthright, Eochaidh's queen secretly conveyed the baby Neil out of the palace of Tara and left him to his fate on a cold hillside. There the hapless infant was discovered by Torna, the illustrious bard of Munster. Torna took care of the child and raised him up until it was time for him to be presented to his father. In time Neil was elected Ard-Righ, or High-King, of Erin. Neil died in A.D. 405, the result of an arrow wound, and was succeeded by his son Eoghan. He died in 465 to be succeeded by his son Muirdeach, followed by the Great Muirceatach, a king who fought many battles and is associated with the ancient Lia Fail, or Stone of Destiny, on which the kings of

Scotland were traditionally crowned. The Lia Fail was first transferred to Scotland's old seat of government at Dunstaffnage Castle in Argyll. Later it found its way to Scone, near Perth, where it was "reverently kept for the consecration of the Kings of Alban", until Edward I carried it off to Westminster in 1296. Current traditions in Scotland suggest that Edward ran off with a substitute stone; or that the stone which was returned in 1951 (when it was removed from Westminster by a number of young Scots) was yet another substitute. The real stone is supposed to be carefully buried in a hillside in Argyll. It may yet be revealed when the proposed Scottish Assembly is established in Edinburgh.

TWO

Clan Feuds

From the times when families of some significance became established in the Highlands and Islands there has been a history of bloodshed in which both guilty and innocent alike have paid the full price of ambition, revenge and jealousy. The origins of many clan feuds were based on quite trivial matters; but, because honour or such-like was involved, what affected, say, a chief, though the latter might be in the wrong, affected the whole clan, and situations which might have been resolved by negotiation, or by the payment of guilt money, as was the case in an older Celtic society, were allowed to magnify themselves with each succeeding generation until, literally centuries after the event, sides were always drawn when two opposing clans met by accident.

To us in the twentieth century, those bad old days might seem to be far removed from the present state of civilization. But even in our perhaps more settled times, violence simmers very close to the sub-surface of most societies which requires little to spark it off. Indeed, the increasing violence of recent years is becoming an aspect of modern life and living which, because of its ubiquity, is also on the way to becoming acceptable by society's tolerance of it. If we in the twentieth century feel this mood of acceptance, as we stand on one side while polarized factions come to grips with each other, how much easier it is to understand conditions some centuries ago when restraints such as law and order were little more than a philosopher's ideal for a Utopian society.

The old house of the MacSorlie chiefs was once situated in Glen Nevis, though there are now no traces of the site. Close by, however, is Dun Dige (Moat Hillock), the site of one of the numerous instances of clan feuds and incidents in Highland history. At one time, one of the MacSorlie chiefs wished to make peace with his old enemies, the Clan Chattan (Mackintosh), and invited some of its senior members to a meeting at his home to discuss possible peace moves and terms; his action, however, was not to the liking of many of the clan, but they toed the line reluctantly. The meeting duly took place and lasted most of the day, at the end of which a large area of common ground was identified and matters looked very good for the cessation of internecine activities between the two clans. In the evening, MacSorlie called on his piper to give the Clan Chattan representatives a good send-off, meaning to sweeten the proceedings further with good entertainment. However, the piper, a man of fixed views, little imagination, and absolutely no flair for diplomacy, proceeded to play a tune which was insulting to the Clan Chattan. Taken aback, and refusing to be placated by the apologies of the MacSorlie chief, the Clan Chattan delegation left the house swearing vengeance.

A little way from the house, at the hillock known as Dun Dige, they stopped and resolved that revenge needed to be swift and carried out that same night. The MacSorlies, thinking that the Clan Chattan were well on their way to their own lands for reinforcements, slept well—too well, however, for, during the hours of darkness, the armed members of the Mackintosh fell on the sleeping inmates of the houses in the Glen, and killed or wounded every man, woman and child they could find. They then set fire to the houses. The MacSorlie chief was one of the first to be killed, but the infant heir escaped with one of the clansmen who, at the same time, took a few of the family heirlooms, including a silver spoon. Fleeing to a cave farther up the Glen, the clansman took care of the child and, when the coast was clear, went to a part of the north of Scotland where the Clan Chattan were not welcome. There the young MacSorlie was fostered until he grew up into a sturdy lad before being taken back into Lochaber by his faithful clansman. Disguising himself as a beggar, the latter called at the house of Inverlair, where the sister of the murdered chief lived. Asking for food, some porridge was brought and, to the amazement of the lady of the house, he proceeded to feed the boy with a silver spoon. At once the family heirloom was recognized and, on closer inspection, she saw the family likeness in the boy's face. On production of other items of identity, the clansman proved the boy's claim to the chiefship; the latter was taken into the household and educated. On reaching seventeen he was installed as Chief of Glen Nevis. After the massacre, no MacSorlie chief would allow a cat in their house, the cat being the emblem of Clan Chattan, whose successors are the present Clan Mackintosh.

On the northern outskirts of Inverness lies the small and picturesque village of Clachnaharry, still reasonably intact despite the urban sprawl from Inverness; it still exudes the atmosphere and character of the fishing village it once was. Its main claim to fame goes back to a desperate battle fought here in 1333, between the Clan Chattan and the Munroes of Foulis, in Ross-shire. The cause of the battle lay in the insulting of John Munro of Foulis, at Strathardle in Perthshire, when he was returning home from Edinburgh with a band of his retainers. While resting at night, the owner of the field where they were encamped cut off the tails of their horses. Munro, determined on revenge, made all possible haste to Ross-shire where he selected about 400 of his most powerful and fearless followers, and returned to Strathardle where he proceeded to devastate the countryside, killing many of the natives and carrying off all the cattle. In this drastic manner insult was avenged. However, more trouble was piling up ahead for Munro. Passing through Moy, Inverness-shire, the home of the Mackintosh, the latter, who had nursed a grudge against Munro for some time, decided it was time to capitalize. He demanded from Munro half of the Strathardle spoils. Munro, in defiance, refused to part with one piece of his hard-won loot and proceeded north. Thus snubbed in public, the Mackintosh gathered some of his henchmen and pursued Munro, overtaking them at Clachnaharry. A bloody engagement took place, with no quarter asked for or given. Soon, however, the Mackintosh had cause to regret his hasty decision, for he and most of his men were killed. The locality of the skirmish is commemorated by a large column erected on top of the rock nearby. Clachnaharry means 'The Watchman's Stone' on which, in olden times, the Magistrates of Inverness had a guard stationed to give early notice of any hostile approach from the north.

For generations a long feud continued between the Camerons and the Mackintoshes. Under an old grant from the Scottish Crown, Mackintosh claimed to be owner of the lands in Lochaber occupied by the Camerons; the latter naturally denied the validity of the grant and refused to pay any rent. Mackintosh's response to this defiance was to collect by poinding and distraining. The Camerons, for their part, opposed force with force and the affair resulted in a number of bloody frays of which the Battle of Invernahavon was one. It is said to have been fought in 1386, on the plain of Invernahavon, where the River Truim flows into the Spey, a little above where the railway now crosses this river.

The event leading to this particular encounter was the uplifting of Cameron cattle by Mackintosh, which the Camerons naturally wished to get back. They marched in force into Badenoch to make reprisals. Mackintosh, being forewarned of the march of the Cameron men, hastened to ask for help from the Laird of Cluny, Chief of the Macphersons. The latter declined, because Mackintosh claimed to be the overall chief of all Clan Chattan, to which both Mackintoshes and Macphersons belonged.

Mackintosh was thus forced to meet the angry Camerons by himself and the ensuing battle was both bitter and bloody, with the Camerons emerging as the victors. The defeated clan fled along the low grounds south of the Spey, pursued by Camerons, until a halt was called for on the height of Briagach, opposite Ballychroan. In desperate plight this time, Mackintosh once more asked Cluny Macpherson to help, offering to relinquish his own claim to the chiefship of all Clan Chattan. Macpherson, who lived a few miles from Invernahavon, agreed and he sent a fresh force of men against the Camerons. The latter, now tired out from marching and fighting, fled, unwilling to face a new enemy. They crossed the Spey near Noidmore and made for their own country by the shortest and safest route through Glen Banchor, hotly pursued by the Macphersons. Though they suffered little from the Macphersons, they were harassed by the country folk who attacked them in their flight and slew a number of them. One of the Camerons who met his death was a chief, killed on the rise known as Torr Thearlaich, the Hill of Charles.

In the course of time the Camerons recovered to plan reprisals and once again invaded the lands of Mackintosh. On this occasion they succeeded in carrying away all the cattle they could find, and unopposed at that. However, Fate, as unpredictable as usual, stepped in and allowed folly to intrude in the plans of the successful Camerons. Returning to their own clan lands, they decided to give vent to their hostile feelings towards Clan Ranald of Keppoch, whose family they deemed intruders in Lochaber. They resolved to send him an insulting message, but found difficulty in getting a man among them who would beard the Keppoch lion in his den. However, one brave and foolhardy soul offered to convey the message on condition that he would get a double share of the loot. This was agreed, and the Cameron man, known as the Slender Tailor, reached the home of Clanranald and delivered the message. Unfortunately for the Camerons a large number of Clanranald's men were gathered to meet him at the time. Enraged by the insult, his men set off and met up with the Camerons, who, completely unprepared for such an immediate reaction and powerful onset, were routed and completely defeated, losing their Mackintosh plunder which now fell into the hands of the MacDonalds of Clanranald, who were more pleased with their good fortune.

As for the Slender Tailor, having delivered the message, Keppoch gave him a start: "If you escape well and good; if not you fail and fall". But the tailor, as smart as his trade, eluded the horsemen following him and crossed through the large peat bog that lies to the north-west of Keppoch House, leaving a furious enemy behind him.

For many generations the powerful Cummings inhabited the wild fastness of early Strathspey and Badenoch. One of the clan even laid claim to the throne of Scotland and afterwards, having entered into a mutual bond with King Robert the Bruce for the deliverance of their common country, Scotland, betrayed him to King Edward of England. Bruce, however, managed to get away from the English Court and, meeting the deceitful Cumming in the Church of the

Grey Friars, in Dumfries, on 10th February 1305, charged Cumming, or Comyn as he was called, with treachery to himself and his country. In return for an insulting answer, Bruce stabbed the Comyn on the steps of the high altar, a deed which haunted Bruce for the rest of his life.

The Cummings and the Shaws were always at feud with each other; the latter clan, being the weaker, at least in numbers, always came off the worse of any encounter. On one occasion their chief was murdered leaving his only child, a boy of a few months, who escaped in the charge of a female member of the Clan Shaw, who took him to the safekeeping of the Laird of Strathardle in the Highlands of Perthshire. After an exhausting journey, she arrived safely and the baby was made welcome; eventually he grew up as the young and rightful heir of Rothiemurchus.

In time young Shaw went back to his clan lands to discover that his adversaries, the Cummings, were on a foraging expedition in the south, and that they were due to return in a few days. Shaw decided that Fate had given him a unique opportunity to avenge the death of his father and his clansmen. The following day Shaw and some worthy men took up a position of watch on the Callort Hill, at the eastern extremity of Rothiemurchus, situated between the two roads leading from Strathspey; they waited. The Cummings were eventually seen coming up the Strath in small parties, each driving a herd of cattle before them. One by one, each party was surprised and killed with little effort on the part of the Shaws, until not one Cumming was left alive. They were all buried on the spot which is now called Lag na Cuimeanach, the Hollow of the Cummings.

The Cummings, completely shattered by the experience, got the message and relations between the two clans improved for some time while Shaw was able to take peaceful possession of his clan lands. But storm clouds were gathering in the form of Shaw's mother, who had survived the earlier massacre and, during the infancy of her son, had assumed general leadership of the Shaws, under the watchful eye of the Cummings. She had married again, to a man called Dallas, a 'southron'. Young Shaw accepted that this move of his mother's was due to her straitened circumstances and,

c

indeed, went so far as to offer the pair residence in his own house at Doune. But the young chief had difficulty in concealing his animosity towards his father-in-law, until one day matters came to a head when, in the presence of a large company, the two men exchanged remarks which were rather near the bone. A short time later Shaw found himself in the sole company of his father-in-law and promptly stabbed him to death, at a place known as Lag an Dalasaich (the Hollow of Dallas). Not satisfied with the murder he severed the head from the body and, carrying the dripping trophy to his mother, threw it at her with taunts that revealed his true feelings about his mother's second marriage.

His mother, after her initial shock, decided on revenge and managed, through her influence, to have the young chief proclaimed outlaw. His whole property, rights and possessions then reverted to the Crown. He died soon afterwards of a broken heart, despised by friends and foes alike. His heritage has continued since to be the property of the Lairds of Grant who, for a mere nominal sum, bought the forfeiture from the Crown.

Typical of the extended militant relationships which existed between the clans were the affairs of the Mackenzies of Gairloch and the MacLeods, who held the ascendancy in Skye, Lewis and Raasay, and on the mainland. In the earlier part of the fifteenth century, Gairloch belonged to the MacLeods and was in the jurisdiction of one Allan MacLeod whose family had close connections with the MacKenzies. Two brothers of MacLeod of Lewis took an oath between them that no person with a drop of MacKenzie blood in him should ever succed to Gairloch and, to ensure that the MacLeod line would remain intact, they landed on the shores of Gairloch after crossing the Minch. But Allan MacLeod had got wind of their intentions and took steps to protect his wife and family by installing them in a stronghold on an island in Loch Tollie, close to the Gairloch/Poolewe road. The Lewis MacLeods, through intelligence brought to them by scouts, found out that Allan MacLeod had gone fishing on the River Ewe. They traced his steps and found him asleep on the river bank, at Cnoc na Michomhairle (the Knoll of the Bad Advice) and at once made him "short by the head". They then made their way to Loch Tollie, burst in on the new-made widow and killed Allan MacLeod's two young sons; a third lad was fortunately absent.

Immediately the cry for revenge went up and Eachainn Ruadh, Red Hector, was sent by his grandfather, Alexander the Sixth of Kintail, to Edinburgh to report the crime and to present evidence in the form of the murdered lads' bloodstained shirts. The Crown gave Hector a commission of fire and sword against the MacLeods and, in addition, a Crown Charter of the lands of Gairloch in his own favour. The two murderers were found soon afterwards and killed without mercy. But it took Hector Roy some years, with his small army of Kintail men, to remove all the settling MacLeods from the Gairloch district.

In particular, the MacLeod stronghold in Gairloch of the Dun or fort on the rocky peninsula, not far from the present Gairloch parish church, held on for a long time and a number of incidents have passed into the legends of both clans. One morning, Eachainn Ruadh had reason to believe that some of the principals of the MacLeods at Dun were to make a journey south, passing the small Bay of Ceann t-Saill; so he decided to lay in wait. The MacLeods little suspecting that their plans were known to their enemies, came along singly, and as each one passed, Eachainn stabbed him with a dirk, hid the body, and waited for the next one, until his 'bag' was three MacLeods before breakfast, a deed which gave him revenge for the murder of his little nephews. From then on, and from time to time, the MacLeods made attempts to regain Gairloch, as is demonstrated from the following take recounted in *The History of the MacKenzies*:

A considerable number of the younger MacLeods who were banished from Gairloch were invited by their Chief to pass Hogmanay night in the Castle of Dunvegan. In the castle kitchen there was employed an old woman known as Mor Bhan (Fair Sarah), who was usually occupied in carding wool and was generally supposed to be a witch. After dinner the men began to drink heavily, and when they had passed some time in this occupation, they sent down to the kitchen for Mor Bhan. She at once joined them in the Great Hall and, having drunk one or two glasses along with them, she remarked that it was a very poor thing for the MacLeods to be deprived of their own lands in Gairloch and to have to live in comparative poverty in Raasay and the Isle of Skye. "But," she said to them, "prepare yourselves and start tomorrow for Gairloch, sailing in the black birlinn (war-boat) and you shall regain it, and I shall be a witness of your success when you return."

The men trusted her, believing she had the power of divination. In the morning they set sail for Gairloch. The black galley was full of MacLeods. It was evening when they entered the loch. They were afraid to land on the mainland, for they remembered the descendants of Domhnall Greannach (Rough Donald, a celebrated Macrae) were still there, and they knew the prowess of the Kintail men only too well. The MacLeods, therefore, turned to the south side of the loch, and fastened their birlinn to the Fraoch Eilean (Heather Island) in the sheltered bay beside Lean nan Saighead (Slab of the Arrows), between Shieldaig and Badachro. Here they decided to wait until morning, and then disembark and walk round the head of the loch. But all their movements had been well and carefully watched. Domhnall Odhar and his brother Iain, the celebrated Macrae archers, recognised the birlinn of the MacLeods and determined to oppose their landing. They walked round the head of the loch by Shieldaig and posted themselves before daylight behind the Leac, a projecting rock overlooking Fraoch Eilean. The steps on which they stood at the back of the rock can still be seen. Domhnall Odhar, being of smaller stature, took the higher of the two ledges and Iain took the lower. Standing on these, they crouched down behind the rock, completely sheltered from the enemy, it commanding a full view of the island, while they were quite invisible to the MacLeods on the island.

As soon as the day dawned the two Macraes directed their arrows on the strangers, of whom a number were killed before their comrades were even aware of the direction from which the messengers of death came. The MacLeods endeavoured to answer their arrows, but, not being able to see the foe, their efforts were of no effect. In the heat of the fight, one of the MacLeods climbed up the mast of the birlinn to discover the position of the enemy. Domhnall Odhar perceiving this, took deadly aim at him when near the top of the mast and 'sent a pin through his broth'.

The slaughter continued, and the remainder of the MacLeods hurried aboard their birlinn. Cutting the rope, they turned their heads seawards. By this time, only two of their number were left alive. In their hurry to escape they left all the bodies of their slain companions unburied on the island. A rumour of the arrival of the MacLeods had during the night spread through the district, and other warriors, such as Fionnladh Dubh na Saigheada and Fear

Shieldaig, were soon at the scene of the action, but all they had to do on their arrival was to assist in the burial of the dead Mac-Leods. Pits were dug, into each of which a number of bodies were thrown, and mounds raised over them which remain to this day, as anyone landing on the island may observe.

Almost the last fight with the MacLeods occurred when Murdoch MacKenzie and several men from Gairloch sailed to the Isle of Skye in a vessel loaded with wine and provisions, with the intention of securing in marriage the daughter and heir in line of Donald MacLeod; the purpose of the visit was to try to put an end to the troublesome dispute. In any event, things went wrong from the start and the voyage proved disastrous. The ship found its way, whether intentionally on the part of the crew, or forced by a great storm, to the sheltered bay of Kirkton of Raasay, opposite the present mansion-house where young MacGilliechallum of Raasay was in residence. Anchor was cast, and young Raasay, hearing that Murdoch MacKenzie was on board, visited the ship on friendly terms. The ulterior motive was, perhaps, to parley with MacKenzie to secure the release of John MacLeod, a kinsman held prisoner in Gairloch; if that failed, then to secure MacKenzie as a prisoner and get an exchange of both hostages. Leaving word on shore that men should be made ready to go to his assistance if things did not go well, young Raasay was rowed across to MacKenzie's ship.

MacKenzie received the MacLeod visitors in the most hospitable and unsuspecting manner and supplied them with as much food and wine as they could consume. In time the party became quite tipsy, save four of MacKenzie's men who, suspicious of the intentions of the MacLeods, retired below to remain both sober and watchful. At last MacLeod, thinking the time was ripe for putting his cards on the table, announced his intention of taking Mac-Kenzie prisoner. Immediately MacKenzie was on his feet, but not before a MacLeod had lodged a dirk in MacKenzie's ribs. The latter, excited by pain, drew his sword but his foot caught on an obstruction on the deck and he fell overboard. He was, however, a strong swimmer and made for the shore, but there was attacked by some MacLeods who had rowed out. They pelted MacKenzie with stones until, his head shattered, he disappeared beneath the waves. Meanwhile, the four MacKenzies who had kept themselves sober, decided to exact the maximum payment for the treachery. Fighting like heroes they killed young Raasay and other important MacLeods and, with the help of the ship's crew, managed to make good their escape to tell the tale of their unhappy venture. Eventually matters became a little more peaceful, but for many generations after that event MacLeod was an unpopular name in Gairloch and district.

Osgood MacKenzie, in his book *A Hundred years in the Highlands* mentions that his grandfather, if he asked a question as to the name of a man, and the man happened unluckily to be a MacLeod, would receive an apologetic answer: 'Le bhur cead Shir Eachainn se Leodach a th-ann' (By your leave, Sir Hector, it is a MacLeod that is in him).

Not all attempts at murder succeeded, as the tradition of MacLeod of Hacklett, in Lewis, goes to show. MacLeod was named Tormod (Norman) and he had the reputation of being one of the bravest warriors the island had seen for a long time. He was closely related to the Chief of the MacLeods of Lewis who had newly married a daughter of MacLean of Duart. One day she took it upon herself to go to Uig, to Tormod MacLeod's farm, to receive the annual dues of a certain number of lambs. She arrived at Hacklett and was received with all the hospitality as befits a visit from a superior. However, by accident or design, one of the good lady's pages tripped up a small stool on which Tormod was sitting. The great man fell to the ground with a thump and was made to look foolish and ridiculous. But the wanton page paid dear for the affront. No sooner had MacLeod raised himself up from the floor when he dealt such a blow to the page with his hand that he fell dead.

The lady, in a fit of rage and frenzy, made off for Stornoway to her husband's castle and swore that she would not be satisfied until MacLeod of Hacklett was killed and all his goods destroyed. Besotted as he was with his new wife, and notwithstanding his close relationship with the intended victim, MacLeod sent twelve men to be the ruin of Hacklett. But, with only one manservant, Tormod was a match for them and killed eleven of MacLeod's men, allowing one to return to Stornoway to tell the tale and report the fate of his fellows.

The Chief then sent another party of twelve, which met with exactly the same fate. By this time the Chief's wife was highly incensed and she sent word to Duart, to her father and brother, relating the assaults on her honour and her position. So from Duart sailed a ship with two dozen chief warriors and some inferior men, all well-armed, and all intent on taking satisfaction from Tormod MacLeod. In time the ship reached Loch Roag, on the west coast of Lewis, and anchored off Loch Tornish, opposite Hacklett. Twelve archers and a mailed soldier landed on the shore. On seeing them MacLeod asked his man-servant which he would prefer to tackle and got the reply that he would rather attempt to repel the twelve men, to save the house from being set on fire. So MacLeod and his servant, the latter no mean fighter himself, set off for the shore, where by this time one batch of MacLeans had landed. A party set off for MacLeod's house but were met by a hail of arrows, each of which found a deadly home in a MacLean. Well pleased with himself, the servant went off to give his master a hand if needed. He found him engaged in stalemate sword-play, for the mailed Mac-Lean combatant was well protected and had his back against a large rock, and was fending off all the sword-moves made by Mac-Leod. MacLeod, more frustrated than desperate, shouted to the servant to think up some way to defeat the enemy, whereupon the servant vanished to reappear on top of the rock with a huge stone which he let drop onto the head of the armoured MacLean, who had not expected an attack from above.

Watching the fighting from the ship, Chief MacLean ordered more men ashore, but they too were met with a hail of arrows until all were killed. Soon, only three men were left on the ship with their chief, who later went ashore unmolested to pick up his dead. Mac-Leod of Hacklett reckoned that after the ship set sail, it would go south and anchor off some suitable spot to bury the dead MacLeans. Sure enough, MacLeod followed the ship from the shoreline until it anchored at Caolas Shader, in the Sound of Harris. Early next morning, MacLeod walked on the shore opposite the vessel. Supposing him to be one of the tenants of that part of the country, he was hailed by a MacLean to know if permission could be had to bury their dead. MacLeod replied, in the affirmative, but asked the master of the vessel to come up on deck so as to speak with him. When the MacLean chief came up MacLeod shouted for him to stand with his back to the mast, so that he might hear him better. The MacLean did this and was thus taken by complete surprise when an arrow from MacLeod's bow fixed him to the mast, killing him. Thus it was that MacLean of Duart, his son and upwards of thirty of MacLean warriors lost their lives. MacLeod returned home to Hacklett to be left alone by the Chief of the Lewis MacLeods and his spiteful wife. Shortly afterwards the MacKenzies gained possession of the island of Lewis, but MacLeod remained at Hacklett, despite his past reputation, until he died an old man.

During the long-continued feuds between the MacLeods and the MacDonalds, the little island of Pabbay, in the Sound of Harris, was the scene of a particularly harrowing incident. One day the inhabitants found to their horror that a large party of MacDonalds was approaching in war galleys, with the evident intention of sacking the island, which was a fertile garden in the sea. The MacLeods on the island, knowing they were too weak to meet the assailants, resorted to stratagem. They collected the women and children and hid them in places of safety round the island some distance removed from the island's little township. They then hid themselves among rocks and clefts in the cliffs, around the shores, from where they watched the progress of the MacDonalds as they landed. The latter made for the township which they found deserted. Pleasantly surprised, they fell to and made themselves comfortable, eating, drinking and collecting as much booty as they could carry.

Meanwhile, the MacLeods rushed the MacDonald boats left on the beach with only a small guarding party. The latter were overcome easily and the craft pushed out into the waters of the Sound which carried them away from the island. Hurrying to their own boats, the MacLeods rowed quickly to the neighbouring island of Berneray and sought the assistance of their kinsmen there, explaining that the MacDonalds were trapped with no means of retreat. The MacLeods of Berneray, keen to get at the mutual enemy, went back to Pabbay Island in strength.

On landing they made for the pillar of smoke that now rose

from the deserted township. Only the church and a large house were standing. The township itself was in ruins. The MacDonalds had gathered in the remaining house, sorting out all the valuable booty, while a small party was sent down to the shore with a drove of cattle. The MacLeods fell on the MacDonalds with black revenge in their hearts. The sight of their burning homes was enough to tune them into the right mood for recompense in blood and death. The MacDonalds, realizing they were fighting for their lives, resisted the MacLeod attacks and made for their beached boats, only to find them gone and in their place the well-guarded craft of the MacLeods. Thus hemmed in between two enemy sides the MacLeods stood their ground for a while until each man of them threw themselves into the sea and drowned, preferring a watery grave to the dishonour of defeat. Not a single man of the invaders remained alive to tell the tale; it was left to the MacLeod sennachies, traditional storytellers, to place the incident in the folk tradition of the Western Isles.

In the middle years of the nineteenth century a number of human bones were discovered in the ground on Pabbay, supposed to have belonged to some of the MacDonalds who fell in the conflict. It is said that there were also found near the same place eight silver rings, a brass cup and a sword of a very ancient make; at the same time and spot the bones of a female were uncovered. This woman was supposed to have been the wife of the leader of the MacDonald band who, not anticipating the terrible outcome of the raid, had accompanied her husband to Pabbay to see the speedy manner in which his band would make an end of the MacLeods—an entertainment which cost her dear.

The small island of Eigg lies off the peninsula of South Morar. Typically, and in common with many other parts of the Highlands and Islands, this basalt-based island of high potential fertility has been allowed to go almost to dereliction. However, in historical times it provided a good environment for the Clanranald family of MacDonalds, who were in perpetual conflict with the MacLeods of Skye. One incident in this relationship, if such it can be called, occurred in 1577, inside a cave known as Uamh Fhraing, the 'Ribbed Cave'. Many versions of the story are told, with two of ancient standing which accord with traditional accounts and so can be accepted as being virtually true. The Old Statistical Account for Scotland (1799) gives us a fairly detailed telling:

At no great distance east of this cave (Uamh a Chrabhaidh) is Uamh Fhraing, remarkable not only for its form, but also for the murder of the inhabitants of this island by Alistair Crotach, Laird of Mac-Leod. The entrance of this cave is so small that a person must creep on four for about twelve feet; it then becomes pretty capacious, its length being 213 feet, breadth twenty-two, and height seventeen. With regard to the murder . . . it is said that some of MacLeod's vassals, returning from Glasgow, touched at the harbour of Eigg. Some Eigg women were then tending cattle in Eilean Chastall, the small island which forms this harbour. The strangers visited and maltreated the women. Their friends having got information, pursued and destroyed those strangers. Very properly, the MacLeods were punished by the Eigg men and bound hand and foot and sent adrift on the sea, to be picked up by friends from Skye.

This treatment of his vassals MacLeod considered as an insult, and came in force to avenge their deaths. The inhabitants, appraised of their danger, flocked to Uamh Fhraing for concealment, excepting three who took other places of refuge.

MacLeod, after landing, having found no inhabitants, believed they had fled to the mainland and resolved to return immediately to Sky. The people in the cave, impatient of their confinement, sent a scout to reconnoitre, who imprudently shewed himself upon an eminence, when he was readily observed by the enemy then actually under sail for Sky. Unfortunately for the inhabitants there was new snow laid upon the ground. MacLeod re-landed and traced the scout to the cave's mouth. He offered, upon delivering up to him the murderers of his people to spare the other inhabitants. The terms were rejected, upon which MacLeod smoked them all to death. In the confined air of this cave the bones are still pretty fresh; and some of the skulls entire, and the teeth in their sockets. About forty skulls have been lately numbered. It is probable a greater number was destroyed; if so, their neighbouring friends may have carried them off for burial in consecrated ground.

In an old MS, the date of the atrocity and the number killed is given: "There are many caves under the earth in the isle which the country people retire to with their goods when invaded, which proved fatal to them in the year 1577, where 395 persons, men, wives and bairns, were smoked with putting fire to the caves." In later years the floor of the cave was cleared of bones, many of the latter being removed as gruesome mementoes by tourists.

This type of atrocity was not unusual in the Highlands. Resulting from the Eigg massacre, a party of MacDonalds carried out retaliatory action on the MacLeods with the burning of Trumpan Church in Skye during a morning service. And, in the early years of the seventeenth century, a party of MacDonalds went to the Church of Gilliechriost in Ross-shire, to burn MacKenzies at their worship, a particularly nasty affair which had long-lasting repercussions.

There are many instances of bloody acts committed with inhuman ferocity in the history of the Highlands; few, however, can match the scene which occurred at the ancient chapel of Gilliechriost, in the Parish of Urray, in Ross. The background to the affair was a quarrel between two chiefs: MacKenzie of Kintail and Macdonnell of Glengarry, who were in dispute over the possession of land. In the development of the dispute the chiefs' underlings took matters into their own hands, feeling that their clans' honour was at stake. The Macdonnells having already made several raids on MacKenzie country, the MacKenzies, for their part, were not disposed to leave wrongs undone, and retaliated by the spoiling of Morar with a large and overwhelming force. Back the Macdonnells went to Kintail of the MacKenzies to wreak further damage to life and property, this time under the leadership of Glengarry's son, Angus. Caught by surprise by this fast and particularly well planned raid, the MacKenzies from Kintail and Lochalsh gathered quickly, but were too late to prevent young Glengarry from escaping to sea with his ships about awash with plunder. Some of the MacKenzies sped to Eilean-donnan, in Loch Duich, while a squad made haste to the narrow strait of the Kyle between Skye and the mainland, through which the Macdonnells, of necessity, had to pass on their return south.

In time the marauding boats were seen; the first was let through unmolested, while the second, a thirty-two-oared galley with the chief's bearings, was attacked. The Macdonnells, surprised, were caught unprepared; all rushed to one side of the heavily-loaded craft, which suddenly overturned and sank to her gunwales. The Macdonnells, floundering in the water, were slaughtered like speared fish; any who reached land were dispatched without quarter given. The body of the young Glengarry was secured and buried in the very doorway of the Kirk of Kintail, so that MacKenzies might trample over it when they went into church.

After that episode, things quietened down to an uneasy simmering; old Donald Gruamach, of Glengarry, died before he could mature plans for the adequate retaliation of the Kyle tragedy and the loss of his son Angus. The new chief of the clan was but an infant. However, a cousin undertook an oath of personal revenge which could be fulfilled only by an act of unequalled magnitude and ferocity. This cousin, MacRanuil of Lundi, had already gained plenty of experience in forays into MacKenzie country, so was an experienced campaigner. These raids, were, however, mere preludes to the final deed in which a solitary life was no compensation, to his way of thinking, for the loss in blood and of land occasioned by the MacKenzies. So he gathered a number of the most ferocious and bloodthirsty of the Macdonnell clansmen whom he force-marched across the hills to arrive at the Church of Gilliechriost on a Sunday afternoon, when it was filled with a crowd of worshippers of the clan MacKenzie.

Without a moment's delay, without a single pang of remorse, and while the small building resounded to the singing of those within, the roof was set on fire. Being thatched, it caught quickly, fanned by a breeze from the east. Soon enough the congregation became conscious of their situation and rushed to the doors and windows, where they were met by a double row of bristling swords. The situation produced a fearful noise. The shrieks of women, the helpless screaming of children, the cries of the infuriated Mac-Kenzie men and the roar of the flames—all these even shook the hearts of the Macdonnells. But not that of Allan Dubh of Lundi. "Thrust them back into the flames, for he that suffers aught to escape alive from Gilliechriost shall be branded as a traitor to his Clan!" At the main doorway MacKenzies were mercilessly killed until their bodies formed a barrier to those inside.

Anxious for the preservation of their children, the scorched mothers threw them from the windows, hoping that the Macdonnells would spare these at least. But it was not to be. At the command of Allan of Lundi, they were received on the points of the broadswords of the men without mercy. Clan honour was at stake and was held in higher esteem than compassion. While the building cracked with the heat, a piper marched round the burning pile playing an extempore pibroch which has ever since been distinguished as the war tune of Glengarry under the title of "Gilliechriost".

Eventually, as the last of the solitary cries were heard, and the last blackened stone toppled to earth from the shattered walls, there was silence. The import of the deed came to the Macdonnells: in less than an hour they had committed the inhabitants of a whole parish to a funeral pyre. They turned south, in two parties, as fast as they could, though having made a long march north, they were exhausted and made little progress. In the meantime the MacKenzies in the district had been roused. Utterly appalled at what had happened, nothing but adequate compensation in deep rivers of Macdonnell blood could satisfy the justified horror in each MacKenzie heart. One body, led by Murdoch MacKenzie of Redcastle, proceeded to Inverness, to follow the first band of fleeing Macdonnells. They caught up with their enemies at Torbreck, in a public house where the latter had stopped to refresh themselves. The house was immediately set on fire and thirty-seven Macdonnells died in the same manner of death as that which they had inflicted on innocent souls earlier the same day.

The second band of Macdonnells, followed closely by Alexander MacKenzie of Coul, chased the other party of Macdonnells, led by Allan of Lundi. Near the hills close by the burn of Aultsigh both met; the Macdonnells, tired and with faint hearts, made for the burn's ford, but in their confusion they missed it and were easily caught and killed. Others, with more physical endurance, coupled with the fear of impending death with no quarter given, sped on as best they could. Allan Dubh of Lundi, seeing the MacKenzies close on his heels, ordered his men to split up, to draw the chase from himself. But the MacKenzies, with a keen nose for their prime victim, glued themselves to his tracks, for

Allan always wore his mark of superiority: a red jacket, symbol of his Captaincy of the Glengarry Macdonnells. In some desperation now, Allan Dubh made for Aultsigh, towards a ravine. There was only one way to escape his pursuers and that was to leap from one side to the other. Only the thought of a sword splitting his head in two was enough to give him both strength and courage to make the leap. He succeeded in clearing the ravine. Behind him, coming up fast, was a young member of the MacKenzie clan. Being athletic and fit he, too, jumped but only touched the opposite side. In desperation, he clung to a slender shoot of hazel bush. Allan Dubh, resting to gather his strength, saw the young lad's attempt and noted his plight. Without a whisper of mercy he took out his sword and slashed the bush. The young man plunged to the bottom and was killed. On the other side of the ravine a Mac-Kenzie musket shot caught Allan Dubh and wounded him. But he managed to make his way down to the shores of Loch Ness, opposite Foyers. He plunged into the loch and began to swim, to be rescued by some of the Frasers of Foyers with whom the Macdonnells were friends. Thus rescued, Allan Dubh escaped the further attention of the MacKenzies. But henceforth the star of the Macdonnells was in the descendant, while that of the MacKenzies waxed. The place on the Aultsigh ravine where the daring leap took place is called Monadh-a-Leumanaich (the Moor of the Leaper). In another version of this tradition, the famous leap is said to have taken place at Ault a Ghiuthais, near Mealfuarvonie, on Lochness-side, the Macdonnells being routed at Lon na Fala (the Bog of Blood). Nearby Ault a Ghiuthais is Creag Giuthas, which to-day has a ravine answering exactly the descriptions in tradition. This ravine is associated with the name Leum a' Cheannaiche, the merchant's leap, on account of the fact that Allan Dubh Macdonnell, the better to acquaint himself with the north country, travelled there before the Gilliechriost raid as a pack-merchant. The raid took place in 1603. The scene of the Macdonnell rout is at the south-east base of Mealfuarvonie; in the vicinity of the Merchant's Leap is an extensive mossy plain which is known as Lon na Fala.

Yet another Leap is associated with a Caithness legend.

This is a tale of excitement and concerns the locale provided by the Dunbeath River, which flows through the Dunbeath Strath in Caithness. At Crageneath, the river is guarded on both sides by perpendicular rock faces, seventy to one hundred feet high; the distance between the two is about thirty-five feet. This gorge is known as the Prisoner's Leap and tradition has it that it was jumped by a man of the sixteenth century, called Ian McCormack Gunn. His mother was a daughter of Clan Gunn, who gave him illegitimate birth and who died shortly after the event. He was brought up by her parents and was commonly known as Ian Mc-Cormack. He grew up to be a sturdy lad and it became evident that he possessed an extraordinary strength. His feats were the talk of the district and some went so far as to say that he had been sent by divine intervention to protect the Clan Gunn against its many enemies. When he grew to manhood he could fell an ox with one blow and he was so swift on foot that he could easily pass a horse at full gallop.

Inevitably Ian was made personal bodyguard to the Chief of the Clan Gunn and accompanied his master into Caithness on all his forays against the Keiths and the Sinclairs. Sometimes in these forays he could wreak havoc among the enemy whether he had a club or a sword in his hand. Indeed it was said that his agility with the sword was such that his opponent could not see the blade. His reputation grew to the extent that the Clan Gunn enemies left them alone and some peaceful years ensued. But the Keiths and the Sinclairs in particular were unhappy about this situation and plotted to get rid of Ian somehow.

The Keiths, who lived in Forse Castle, had their own champion, Angus Mor MacKay. He had been in the service of his chief for many years but was not thought to be much of a match for Ian McCormack. Indeed it was rumoured that MacKay had seen Mc-Cormack in action in battle and had said that it was death for any man to challenge the latter in a straight fight. So the plan was to get Ian alone in the hills and defeat him by sheer power of numbers. Now it was Ian's habit to take to the hills often to walk and hunt. His enemies knew this and decided to keep a close watch on his movements. One day he went for a long walk into the hills around Braemore. This was reported back to the Chief of the

Keiths and plans were laid immediately to capture Ian when he was asleep. The Sinclairs were also told of the plans and between the two clans they moved to Braemore with evil intent. Some forty picked men went on the march to attack the unsuspecting Gunns, while another party crept up on the sleeping Ian and captured him, though not without a great struggle on his part. At last he was overwhelmed and bound hand and foot was taken to Forse Castle. The Chief of the Keiths was overjoyed at the news. He immediately sent for Sinclair of Dunbeath to decide the best way of disposing of McCormack. The Keiths were for hanging him there and then, but advisers were against him coming to any quick decision and said that he should be tried in fair trial. If McCormack was killed for no reason then there would be a general uprising of people in the district for Ian was well liked and had won respect. Thereupon heads were brought together to hatch out some suitable way to get rid of Ian without arousing the idea that he was being killed purely for political reasons.

Eventually it was decided to match Ian McCormack with Angus Mor MacKay, but not in battle; rather an athletic competition was to be arranged. However, the catch in the scheme was that the route was to be arranged beforehand so that if Ian was not to be killed by armed men along the race track he would have to jump over the Crageneath Gorge. No living man had ever jumped that gap and it was certain that McCormack would also fail and be dashed to pieces at the bottom. So it was planned and the following day, when McCormack was brought up from the dungeons of Forse Castle, instead of seeing a gallows he was met with friendliness. He was told that he was to be matched in athletic strength and stamina with Angus Mor MacKay and was promised his life and freedom if he could beat him.

The irons which shackled Ian's hands and feet were struck away and at a signal both men began at a steady pace to make for the decided route across Dunbeath Strath. Though stiff at first from his overnight stay in the dungeon, Ian soon got his circulation going and rallied his body to meet the challenge of Angus Mor, who kept pace with little effort. Then the high ground was reached. Ian slowed down to notice that Angus Mor was gaining ground. In the

Sunset over Loch Voil

(*Above*) looking towards Invernavon battlefield and (*below*) Skye, the Cuillins from Portree

Inverness Castle

Gilliechriost
burial ground

The Prisoner's Leap:
Crageneath Gorge which
Ian McCormack leapt
over to save his life

Forse Castle, former home of the Keiths in Caithness

(*Above*) the Well of the Heads, Loch Oich and (*below*) Glen Shee

(*Above*) the former Milton Inn, Dunbeath, where Glenorchy's men celebrated after the Battle of Altimarlach and (*below*) the Wick River across
which Glenorchy's troops waded during the battle

(*Above*) Stornoway, Lewis and (*below*) the battlefield of Culloden

Glen
Coe

meantime Ian was thinking deeply and asking himself why he was being put to this test when he knew he could have been as easily hanged. All along the route were posted armed Keith and Sinclair guards and Ian soon realized that he was being led to the Crageneath Gorge. He was expected to jump it to gain his life and freedom! It was a matter that gave him concern; it was also a matter of taking the chance or ending his life in a shameful manner. Far better, he thought, to die bravely for his life and reputation than to die with a cowardly blemish on his career. Angus Mor kept a watchful eye on Ian as the two took the rising ground in their stride. Then Ian stopped. Angus Mor carried on, thinking that his opponent was now done for. To his surprise Ian started up again and passed him at speed. Straight for the precipice he went and, with one bound he soared upwards; his kilt seemed to act as wings as he drifted through the air to the other side. He landed, but a few feet short of the rock. Thinking that this was his last minute on earth, he clutched the slender branches of a tree and succeeded in holding on to it. The tree itself held, its roots fortunately anchored deep in a cleft of rock with earth enough for a good root system. Ian then pulled himself up to the top. A hail of arrows came at him like angry wasps from the other side as Clan Keith archers tried to kill him. But he managed to evade them and made his way towards Braemore and safety. After that episode the Gunns were left alone. The raiding party which had been held in readiness to fall on the Gunns were signalled to retreat and the district then had several more years of comparative peace. Ian is said to have lived to a ripe old age and died in his bed, but the story of his feat lived on in tradition.

The last two clan battles fought in the Highlands took place in the Hebrides and were linked by the same feuding clans: Clan MacDonald and Clan MacLeod. The battle on Uist led to the final contest on Skye. The Battle of Carinish took place in 1601, near Teampull na Trionad (Trinity Temple), the ruin of which still stands on a knoll on the Carinish promontory in North Uist. The battlefield is called Feith na Fala, the Field of Blood, and is said to be the scene of the last battle to be fought in Scotland solely with swords and bows and arrows. The cause of the contest was a feud between the MacDonalds of Sleat and North Uist, and the MacLeods of Harris and Dunvegan. The feud reached boiling point when Donald Gorm Mor MacDonald divorced his wife, Mary Mac-Leod, and sent her home. To avenge this insult about sixty Mac-Leod warriors took a boat for North Uist to lay waste the island. They arrived at Trinity Temple to "tak a prey of goods out of the precinct of the church at Kiltrynad wher the people had put all their goods and cattal, as in a sanctuarie".

They were, however, met by sixteen good North Uist Mac-Donalds who literally chopped the MacLeods to pieces in a stiff fight, only two of the latter escaping. A third, Donald Glas Mac-Leod, attempted to escape but was caught and, as tradition has it, hit on the head and killed; he was subsequently buried in the vicinity of the Temple. In 1840 a skull with a gash in it was reported as "lying about in the church". The other dead MacLeods were buried where they fell at Cnoc Mhic Dhomhnuill Ghlais (Hillock of Donald Glas) beside the shore.

This set-back made the MacLeods even more determined to get some kind of revenge; the Clan honour was at stake, as it always was. Opportunity presented itself when a party of MacDonalds was reported as having been seen in Skye, at Coire na Creiche, the Corrie of the Foray. A large number of MacLeods, among whom were MacLeods from Lewis, made preparations to intercept the MacDonalds. It was late in the afternoon when both parties met for battle and tradition relates that the darkness of night echoed with the triumphant yells of the victors and the death-shrieks of the wounded and dying. The tide of battle swirled this way and that with no side giving ground, until it was noticed that the MacLeod ranks had been severely thinned. This gave the MacDonalds renewed courage and by pressing the fight with a ferocity that startled the MacLeods they succeeded in taking some thirty Mac-Leods prisoner, among whom was Rory MacLeod, Chief of the Clan. The rest of the MacLeod force was routed. Afterwards negotiations between the two clans took place to conclude with an end of a feud which had been a tragedy for centuries. The conclusion was an achievement in itself for the relationship between the two clans in previous centuries had been described as "putting rings on each others fingers, and dirks in each others hearts".

The Highlands, generally, were not quite free from feuding, though large-scale battles were finished. Robert Chambers, in his *Domestic Annals of Scotland*, notes that on 9th February 1603, there was "an outbreak of private warfare which throws all contemporary events of the same kind into the shade".

In pursuance of a quarrel of some standing between Clan Gregor and Colquhoun, Laird of Luss, the former came in force to the banks of Loch Lomond. The parties met in Glenfruin, where the Colquhouns, outmanœuvred by their enemies, were overthrown. The MacGregors, besides killing a number of persons, variously stated at three score and more, in the battle, are alleged to have murdered a number of prisoners (amongst whom, by the way, was Tobias Smollet, Bailie of Dumbarton, very likely an ancestor of the novelist, his namesake), and also some poor unarmed people. The whole slaughter is set down at 140 persons. Besides all this they carried off 600 cattle, 800 sheep and goats, fourteen score of horse and mares. It has been alleged that they killed the Laird after taking him prisoner, and murdered a number of schoolboys from the college or school of Dumbarton; but these would appear to be groundless charges.

Such as their guilt was, it proved the commencement of a long course of oppression and misery endured by this clan. According to a contemporary writer, a mournful procession came to Edinburgh, bearing eleven score bloody shirts, to excite the indignation of the king against the MacGregors. There being no friend of the MacGregors to plead their cause, letters of intercommuning were immediately issued against them.

Later in that year, Chambers reports:

Campbell of Ardkinglass, set on by the Earl of Argyll, exerted himself to capture MacGregor of Glenstrae, who, for some months, had been under ban of the government on account of the slaughterous conflict of Glenfruin. He called MacGregor to a banquet in his house, which stands within a loch, and there made no scruple to lay hold of the unfortunate chieftain. Being immediately put into a boat, under a guard of five men, to be conducted to the Earl of Argyll, MacGregor contrived to get his hands loose, struck down the guardsman nearest him, and leaping into the water, swam to land unharmed. Some time after the Earl of Argyll sent a message to MacGregor, desiring him to come and confer with him, under promise to let him go free if they should come to an agreement. The rest is reported by the diarist, Birrel: "MacGregor was convoyit to Berwick by the guard, conform to the Earl's promise; for he promised to put him out of Scots Ground. Sae he keepit ane Hielandman's promise; but they were not directed to part with him, but to fetch him back again. The 18 of January he came at even again to Edinburgh, and upon the 20 day, he was hangit at the Cross, and eleven mae of his friends and name, upon ane gallows; himself being chief, he was hangit at his awn height above the rest of his friends".

In the year 1647, the garrison of Dunaverty Castle, situated at the southern end of the Kintyre peninsula in Argyll, was massacred almost to a man after surrendering to an army of Covenanters. At the time, the massacre attracted little attention: it was seen merely as one of a long and tedious string of incidents in a brutal war between two factions. Indeed, the general opinion in Scotland was that while the massacre was not excusable it was understandable. The background to the affair was the continuing religious disputes in Scotland between Catholic and Presbyterian and, in a wider context, of Covenanter versus Royalist. And, as ever when there is a religious mix to politicking, the opposing sides adopted stances which left little or no room for mercy and tolerance. However, as in many instances of its type in the Highlands and Islands, inter-clan feuding and the bitterness aroused by a great civil war also played their parts.

Central to the massacre was the rivalry between the Campbells and the MacDonalds, which had been nurtured in all its fine details for many generations. By the year 1607 the Campbells, under the Earls of Argyll, had finally triumphed over the southern branch of the MacDonalds, who were driven from Kintyre in that year. A decade later, the MacDonalds also lost Islay, their last major possession in Scotland; many fled to their close kinsmen, the MacDonnells of Antrim in Ulster. Naturally the MacDonalds did not reconcile themselves to this defeat, crushing as it was both territorially and psychologically. Many of their leaders sought some means to repair the damage done to the honour of the clan. Among these was Col MacGillespick, usually known as Col Ciotach. In 1615 Col seized Colonsay and held it, eventually to legalize his position in the 1630s by a lease from the Campbells, though they later ousted Col from this outpost, taking advantage of the confusion of the First Bishops' War in 1639, during which the Campbells from Islay invaded Colonsay, capturing Col and two of his sons.

It was in this way that the age-old conflict between the Campbells and the MacDonalds became a minor element in the greater struggle between King Charles I and the Covenanters who, by 1639, had seized control of Scotland. The 8th Earl of Argyll had managed to become a leading figure among the Covenanters, which fact brought into play changes in the political situation in the southern Highlands. For instance, the Campbell victory over the MacDonalds, which was entirely an inter-clan affair, had been aided by the support of the Crown. Now, however, the Campbells were in conflict with the Crown and were in rebellion. The MacDonalds, seeing the political opportunities, took advantage of the name-changes. The Earl of Antrim, representing the MacDonalds, offered to invade the Argyll lands at his own expense; this plan, however, came to nothing, but it did add its fuel to what was to be a final funeral pyre.

The years of the 1640s saw much bloodshed in Scotland, with each skirmish and battle adding its own due leaven of hatred, on one side for the other. Montrose had his year of victories in 1644–45, aided by Irish troops, in which he defeated six Covenanting armies in turn. But, in September 1645, Montrose suffered defeat at Philliphaugh and was forced to flee to the Highlands. In this and in later successes, the Covenanters put all captured prisoners to death. Irish, papists, women, whatever: they were barely human and needed no trial. However, what the troops of Montrose suffered was little more than they had themselves meted out to the Covenanters.

Thus matters came to a head. A band of Highland rebels found themselves at the tip of Kintyre, locked in Dunaverty Castle, waiting the approach of General Leslie, a veteran of Continental wars and who had led the Covenanters to victory at Philliphaugh. Despite a plea for pardon Leslie advanced to the west. On the 17th May, Leslie began his march and reached Inveraray on the 21st; on or about the 25th he laid siege to Dunaverty Castle. During the month of June several desperate assaults were made on the fortress, but all were repelled with great losses on the side of the assailants. The place was in fact well nigh impregnable and those on the inside could, with plenty of provisions, withstand a year of siege. But by mid-July it was discovered by the besiegers that the water supply to the castle came through pipes connected to a small spring outside the castle walls. These were at once disconnected; a few days later the MacDonald inmates found themselves in a sorry state. With a stone wall landwards and the sea behind them, and with no water save for that collected from passing rain showers, they came to a decision that a conditional surrender should be negotiated. Word was sent to Leslie's troops. But this was rejected with a message to "surrender at discretion or to the mercy of the kingdom".

So the castle inmates, their lives in the hands of their enemies, gave up their arms and became the prisoners of the Covenanters. During the next five days, Leslie was under powerful persuasion from John Nevoy, a minister who had been appointed to act as chaplain to one of the regiments of the army, to kill the Mac-Donalds and members of other clans, such as the MacDougalls, in the detainees. Nevoy borrowed the words of Samuel to press his arguments: "What meaneth then this bleating of the sheep in mine ears and the lowing of the oxen which I hear". And in a long harangue he exhorted the conquerors to finish their work, and threatened their captain with the curse of Saul who spared the Amalekites. The prisoners were then put to the sword or thrown over the cliffs to the rocks below; some were forced to drink sea water. The castle itself was burned to the ground.

The best account of what happened at Dunaverty is contained in an account written by a Henry Guthrie. He was a Covenanter at the time of the massacre, though he was to write his memoirs as a staunch Royalist with a deep hatred of his former colleagues. He claimed that 500 men were massacred after surrendering on the promise that their lives would be spared. General Leslie had been reluctant to allow the massacre, but had been persuaded to order by Argyll and John Nevoy. Guthrie portrays Leslie, Argyll and Nevoy subsequently walking "over the ancles in blood", and

Leslie remarking to Nevoy: "Now, Mr John, have you not once got your fill of blood?" Despite a possible bias on the part of Guthrie, there is little inherently improbable about Guthrie's accounts that 500 men from Dunaverty Castle were "cruellie and unhumanlie butchered in cold blood". Only a child, little John MacDougall, younger of Dunollie, was spared. According to tradition, those given the task of carrying out the execution were Campbells related to women and children who had been herded into a barn and burnt alive on the orders of Alasdair MacDonald. Many of those killed at Dunaverty were MacDonalds.

Later, Leslie crossed to Islay to confront the garrison in Dunyveg Castle, which soon surrendered on promise of quarter. This time the terms granted to the garrison were honoured, but Col Ciotach was later executed on the orders of the Earl of Argyll. Thus did a great national conflict serve to fit pieces into a plan for inter-clan revenge which neither side could have foreseen nor hoped for.

One of the most notable events to occur in Brae Lochaber was the Keppoch murders, committed in 1663. When Donald Glas, 11th Chief of Keppoch died, he eldest son, Alexander, was still a minor. While Alexander and his brother Ranald were completing their education in Rome, the clan was ruled by their uncle, Alasdair Buidhe. Soon after the two lads returned home, Alasdair threw a banquet to celebrate the occasion, at which Alexander assumed his accession to the chiefship of the clan. Among the guests were a father and his six sons, who belonged to a branch of the Keppoch Macdonnells, known as Siol Dughaill, who secretly coveted the chiefship and whose ambitions were encouraged by others.

By a previous arrangement, this family picked a quarrel during the festivities and in the rumpus which followed, the young Alexander was murdered, as was his brother Ranald. Their deaths were announced as an accident, which led to suspicion falling on the uncle, Alasdair Buidhe, who was thought to be guilty of complicity in the crime, though no proof was ever brought out against him.

However, an avenging angel was abroad, in the form of the Keppoch Bard, Iain Lom. When he heard news of the crime he set out for Invergarry, and begged the Chief of Glengarry to take revenge for the deed. But the latter was unwilling to commit himself to any action in view of the lack of evidence that indeed it was a murder. The bard then set out for the Isle of Skye, to plead with Sir James MacDonald of Sleat to avenge the deed. At first Sir James was reluctant to have any part in the case; but Iain Lom insisted, on a number of repeated visits and, at last, in July 1665, two years after the murder, Sir James obtained a commission of fire and sword to avenge it, issued by the State in Edinburgh. He sent fifty men to the mainland who were met and guided by Iain Lom to the house of the murderers at Inverlair, in Glen Spean. But they found the building strongly barricaded. Resistance was beaten down and the whole family was killed in their own house. Iain Lom, feeling particularly vindictive, had the heads cut from the victims' bodies and buried the latter in a knoll at the east end of the present Inverlair Lodge. The heads he strung on a rope of heather and slung them over his shoulder to present his evidence of justice to Macdonnell of Invergarry, who had refused him aid in the first place.

When he was passing close by the side of Loch Oich, he washed the heads in a well located near the shore, which has ever since been named Tobar-nan-Ceann (the Well of the Heads). In 1812 a monument was erected by Alasdair, Chief of Glengarry, over the well to commemorate the gruesome incident. After showing the heads to Glengarry, Iain Lom sent them to Sir James MacDonald as evidence that the deed was complete and that rough justice had been meted out. Honour was now satisfied. The bard later composed a Gaelic lament in memory of the tragedy: "Mort na Ceapaich". It is an interesting sidelight to this event that Iain Lom carried through his search for justice out of loyalty to the Chief, even though his sister was married to the father of the murderers. During the last century, the grave at Inverlair was opened and seven headless skeletons were found, thus dispelling any doubts about the truth of a 200-year-old part of Highland clan history.

The Wardlaw Manuscript is an interesting document containing many highlights of Highland history and refuses to pull the punches when it relates contemporary events, as the following incident shows—all because of a churlish Highlander and a cheese:

Slaughter at Inverness Fair; the Battle of the Cheese, 1665. A Rude riot and slaughter at a fair in Inverness, called Kebbock Day, August

18, being the Feast of the Assumption of the Blessed Virgin. Upon the hill south of the Castle, the house market stands and there being some women upon the edge of the brae, selling cheese and bread, ready for such as could not go far to fetch it, one Finlay Dhu, a townsman, taking up a cheese in his hand, asked what the rate of it was. This being told him, whether designedly or by negligence, he let the cheese drop from his hand and down the hill it runs into the river.

The woman told him she would oblige him to pay; he (a crabbed fellow) gave her cross language in defiance. One that stood by espousing the quarrel, held him fast, and took off his bonnet in pledge until he should pay the woman. A relation of Finlay's challenged this man, as it was none of his concern. To threatening words they go to blows, till at length most of the hill market is engaged in a confusion. This alarms the whole town; the guards are called, who come in arms, and Joe Reed, a pretty man, their Captain, runs in betwixt the parties to separate them. Several others present offer their mediation; but no hearing. Swords are drawn, guns presented and some wounds given. Provost Alexander Cuthbert is told that his guards are not regarded; he puts on a steel cap, sword and targe, causes ring the alarm bell and comes straight to the hill, and many pretty fellows with him. The people cry for justice; the guards, being pressed and abused, let off some shot, and two men are killed outright and above ten wounded. The noise is hushed and matters examined. The guard is blamed. The Provost, in a fury, said he allowed and avowed what was done; for who durst disturb the King's free burgh at a market time?

The Highlanders keep a-brooding. Two Macdonnells were killed, one other and one Philan died of their wounds. The open rupture was closed on both sides with a punctilio of honour; but a revenge was promised and vowed. A great many—Frasers, Grants and Mackintoshes—offered to compose the matter, calling it chance-medley and extenuating him that was the cause of the fray. The leading man of the Macdonnells present were addressed by the Magistrates, and civilly treated with a promise of strict examination and execution of the blood; but alas! it was post maufragium, or a pardon after execution, as the lost party thought. This rupture bursts out afterwards; but the unhappy fellow that occasions the fray was shapen for mischief, being marked for a stigma, having one half of his beard white, the other half black! Meanwhile, the wounded men and the dead corpses were all carried over to this side of the bridge of Ness and into the town. The parishioners of Wardlaw went into the town and transported their corpses to their interment at

Kirkhill, very decently, and the other wounded men also that died, of all of which I was an assisting eye witness.

Another claim to be the last feudal battle to be fought on Scottish soil is the Battle of Altimarlach, near Wick, in Caithness. When George Sinclair, 6th Earl of Caithness died in 1676, he left no male heir to succeed him. Before his death he had been in grave financial difficulties and had sold his estates, and the titles, to Lord Glenorchy, who was one of his principal creditors. Two dispositions were made out in favour of Glenorchy, dated 1661 and 1672, in each of which were conveyed lands and property. The second disposition stated that in the event of non-redemption, Glenorchy and his heirs were to be enabled to assume the surname of Sinclair and wear the arms of the house of Caithness. Glenorchy was known in his time as the Grey Fox, and it was generally thought that he had tricked the Earl of Caithness into putting this particular clause in the disposition. For the remainder of his life, after 1672, George Sinclair received an annuity from Glenorchy. Sinclair's wife was a daughter of the Earl of Argyll and a relation of Glenorchy; after Sinclair died in 1676, Glenorchy married his widow, then the Dowager Countess. He assumed the title of Earl of Caithness, by which time the deed under which he had acquired the estates had been confirmed by Royal Charter under the Great Seal.

However, the method used by Glenorchy to obtain the earldom was not popular and many of the Caithness tenants and landlords actually made known their dislike of him and their support for someone who disputed Glenorchy's right to the title: George Sinclair of Keiss. The dispute was submitted to four of the most distinguished lawyers in Scotland whose decision was in Glenorchy's favour. There was, however, no doubt that Glenorchy had greased the palms of these lawyers and when the King eventually sent a letter to the Privy Council in Edinburgh ordering them to issue a proclamation prohibiting George Sinclair of Keiss from assuming the title Earl of Caithness, the affair was almost confirmed. Sinclair of course paid no attention to the interdict and retained possession of his lands and took every opportunity to enrage Glenorchy's chamberlains, by making it difficult for them to collect the rents. Sinclair was supported in his active opposition by two friends and kinsmen, David Sinclair of Broynach and William Sinclair of Thura. These two gave George all the assistance he required, to the extent of taking part in a raid on Thurso Castle to take possession of it, and nearly razing it to the ground. Glenorchy's answer to this affront was to appeal to the Privy Council, on the grounds that George Sinclair had failed to obey the interdict. On 11th November 1679, the Privy Council passed an Act charging the hail kin, friends and followers of John, Earl of Caithness, to concur and assist in recovering the disputed lands.

In order to put this Act into effect in the summer of 1680, Glenorchy invaded Caithness with 1,100 men. The force was made up of the different branches of Clan Campbell, including Glenlyon, Glenfalloch, Glendochart and Achallander, together with men from the estates of his brother-in-law, the Laird of MacNab. Glenorchy's men were passing through Braemore, on the confines of the county, when George Sinclair was informed of their presence. He immediately made plans to meet Glenorchy in the open field and collected all his followers, some 500 to 800 men. His force consisted of a number of old men, all totally untrained for the proposed encounter. The only person with military training was William Sinclair of Thura, who had served as a major in the German wars.

The two armies met near Stirkoke. However it was near nightfall and Glenorchy refused battle to retire to the hills of Yarrows. The place where the Campbells spent the night was known as Torran na Gael, or the Highlanders' Hill. Glenorchy's main reason for refusing to fight was that he had plans to organize an ambush to catch all the Sinclair army unawares. He sent some officers and scouts out to survey the possibilities.

They found the Burn of Altimarlach, where it joins the north side of the Wick River about two miles west of the town. This is a rather strange watercourse, as it runs for only a distance of two to three hundred yards when it dries up almost completely. Near to where it joins the Wick River there are steep banks which form a gully. The land beside the burn is high and then slopes away towards the river, forming a peninsula. Glenorchy and his officers thought this an ideal site for the ambush and forthcoming battle. The Sinclairs in the meantime had retired to Wick, where Glenorchy had arranged to have an unusual party awaiting them. He had planned that one of his ships laden with whisky should go aground at the mouth of the Wick River. A secret agent of the Campbells gave some of the whisky to the Sinclairs. They then took possession of the ship and spent the night in riotous drinking. The Campbells, for their part, acted prudently and kept themselves sober and awake.

Early next morning, Glenorchy left the hills of Yarrows with his army, the movement of which was reported to the Sinclairs at Wick, where George Sinclair mustered his men, though with great difficulty. His men, as was to be expected, were mostly in a drunken stupor. In great disarray he led them up the Wick River to meet the enemy.

But Glenorchy had prepared for battle some time earlier. He drew up 500 of his men on the flat ground beside the river and ordered the rest of his force to conceal themselves in a gully. When the Sinclairs arrived they made a detour to the right at some distance from the head of the gully and did not see the ambush that was laid for them. The detour was made in order to get the advantage of higher ground and to keep the enemy between them and the river. When the armies were a short distance apart Glenorchy gave the signal for his men to attack and so battle commenced. The Campbells charged furiously against the Sinclairs. The latter, weak as they were after their dissipated night, gave way in their lines and they were driven before the broadswords of the Campbells up the brae towards the Burn of Altimarlach. Then the reserves of Campbells rose up from their ambush position in the gorge and met the Sinclairs face to face.

The Sinclairs were now pressed both front and rear and, in a bid to escape, rushed *en masse* downhill towards the Wick River. They were followed by Campbells who chased them into the water and cut them down until the river's colour turned to red. So many Sinclairs were slain that the Campbells were able to walk dryshod over the river to the other side. A number of the Sinclairs who tried to escape by making a rush for the open plain were cut down by battle axes and broadswords. The leaders, Sinclair of Thura and Sinclair of Keiss, were able to escape because they were on horseback. The battle did not last for more than a few minutes, but in this short space of time more than 200 Sinclairs had died. The battle, if such it can be called, ended in disaster to the county of Caithness, and it was a humiliating blow to the pride of the Sinclairs. After the battle Glenorchy quartered some of his troops in Caithness. They levied rents and taxes on the inhabitants and in general treated them harshly and oppressively as if in a conquered country. But the affair was far from being ended.

Undaunted by the reverse he had suffered at Altimarlach, George Sinclair of Keiss continued his opposition to Glenorchy. In a fresh attempt to resolve his situation by force, he laid siege to Castle Sinclair and took it after some feeble resistance was put up by the defenders. For this, he and his three friends, Sinclair of Thura, Sinclair of Broynach and MacKay of Strathnaver, fell under the ban of the Government and were declared rebels. Afterwards, through the influence of the Duke of York, later James II, George Sinclair finally secured his claim to the Earldom of Caithness and obtained possession of his patrimonial property. The sale of the earldom was classed as an illegal transaction and the decision of the Scottish lawyers in favour of Glenorchy seems very strange. The Earldom of Caithness was a male fee by its original grant, which would seem to be a bar in any way for it being gifted or disposed of to a stranger, and even of the king altering its tenure, where there was no previous forfeiture. Glenorchy was Earl of Caithness for about six years and, as compensation for his loss, was created Earl of Breadalbane and Baron of Wick. But he was always detested by the people of Caithness who regarded him as a military butcher and never forgave him for the slaughter of their kinsmen at Altimarlach.

Glenorchy, the Grey Fox, was a cunning man, devious and as slippery as an eel. In 1692 he became implicated in organizing the Massacre of Glencoe, and for that treacherous deed an action of high treason was raised against him. He was committed to prison in Edinburgh, where he remained for some time; but he was eventually released without being brought to trial.

The site of the Battle of Altimarlach is marked by a large Celtic cross bearing the inscription: "The Battle of Altimarlach was fought around this spot, 13th July 1680. The last feudal battle in Scotland. Erected 1901." In 1976 plans were made to make the site of the battle more accessible to tourists and the public, by a footpath from Wick to the battlefield.

During the seventeenth century there raged a bitter feud between the Frasers of Lovat and the men of Atholl in Perthshire. Following a terrible raid by the latter into the Lovat country, during the absence of nearly all its male inhabitants engaged on a similar expedition elsewhere, the Frasers returned to find their houses pillaged and burned, their women and children slain or driven away, and their cattle routed by the invaders. Viewing the scene, they vowed terrible revenge and called upon the laird, Lord Lovat, to lead their expedition south. Lovat, a man of fierce passions, swore solemnly on the crosshilt of his dirk that he would not return to his own lands again until he had either captured or put to death every living creature in the Atholl country. So the Fraser clan were at once marshalled and they set their stern faces towards the south.

Making rapid progress they were fortunate enough to find the Atholl country quite unprotected, and for two whole days they harried, burned and slaughtered to their fill. At last they gathered their plunder and made for home. But just before they set off, leaving the land blackened and bloodied, a cock was heard to crow from some deserted farmhouse a long distance behind them. Faint though the sound was it reached the sharp ears of Donald Fraser, the henchman of Lord Lovat and he at once reminded his chief that his vow had not been fulfilled to the last letter. Any oath taken on the dirk was then considered to be the most binding of any and because it was a crime against honour to break such an oath, Lovat ordered Donald to go back with a small party of men and not to return until the cock had been killed.

As Donald's party traced their way back to the farmhouse, they were suddenly attacked by some furious Atholl men, who were only too glad to make the most of the opportunity for revenge. In no time at all, the Frasers were cut to pieces with Donald himself left the only survivor, being overpowered and bound tightly. He was then forced by threats to guide the Atholl men back to where the Frasers were temporarily encamped. But he refused and, though subjected to torture, he held true. Then, in a superhuman effort, he broke his bonds and made off for his life. But before he had got a hundred yards he was overtaken and killed on the spot. Faced now with a problem, the Atholl men resorted to strategy. They put on the tartans of the dead Frasers and traced the tracks of Donald's party. Then, with a small band, equal in number to that of the now-dead Frasers, the Atholl men moved northwards while the main body followed some distance in the rear.

After marching two or three miles they came in full view of the Frasers, encamped in a little hollow on the side of a hill. Feasting on plundered meat, the Frasers were unaware of their being discovered and were quite unprepared for attack. The main body of the Atholl men having assembled, they surrounded the hill. The Frasers, seeing a small body approach, in their tartan, hailed them. Their surprise was great when the Fraser kilts were cast aside and there were revealed wild Atholl men charging down on the camp, intent on nothing but killing. The main body of the Atholl men now moved in and proceeded to a task of little short of slaughter and butchery. Lord Lovat was shouting for his horse when he was cut down by several of his opponents at once, each eager for the credit of his death. The rest of the Frasers, after beating off one attack, realized they were outnumbered and fled, leaving the Atholl men to return home with their plundered possessions.

Honour, however, did not desert that field of battle, for the Atholl men generously gave the rites of burial to their fallen foes and erected an immense cairn of stones over the graves, known as Frasers Cairn. And, in the following years, local legend told of the ghost of Lord Lovat which could be seen at midnight rushing madly round the cairn calling loudly for a horse.

THREE

Treachery and Betrayal

It has ever been one of the inborn elements which go to make up the Highland character that hospitality to the stranger at the door is a prime mark of one's civilization. In another context, the humane treatment of one's fellows in their dire straits was accepted as being a normal attitude to living. But Highland history shows that the exceptions have made the rule and has thrown up some examples of vicious and inhuman treatment towards one's fellow men. The best known, perhaps, is the Massacre of Glencoe. Other examples include those where, for personal gain, a chief kidnapped an opponent to keep him in such conditions that death came as a welcome rescuer. Other instances of treachery were not of the making of Highlanders, but were perpetrated by those who bought up the estates of impoverished lairds and clan chiefs and then refused to recognize or subscribe to the idea that possession of land often means possession of those who live on it, and that the purchase of land brings with it a responsibility, perhaps more moral than legal, for its tenants. The treachery which that sad era in Highland history known as 'the Clearances' saw is still remembered. Another kind of treachery was seen after the Battle of Culloden, when the normal codes of conduct, which might have been expected of soldiers, were dismissed on the orders of the Duke of Cumberland, producing an anarchy which resulted in the death of innocents. Many Highlanders who were on the point of death on the field of battle were despatched with the knife and bullet to satisfy the craving for killing which Cumberland's licence had loosed among his troops, including his officers who might otherwise have been anxious to see their commissions kept untainted by an enforced association with a base and basic kind of treachery.

Then there is the affair of the betrayal of Montrose, laid at the door of Neil MacLeod of Assynt, which even today creates some controversy, recent evidence however suggests that MacLeod was quite innocent of the actual betrayal, though he was in a degree party to those who caused it. This chapter deals with some classic examples of treachery in all stations of Highland life; but let it be said that these examples are only typical highlights of the times in which they were committed and that in general a high respect for life was held by the more common folk.

In the early history of the Highlands, the Clan MacDonald held a prominent and dominant position, both as regards their numbers and the extent of the territory they held. For instance, at one time the clan held sway from the Island of Lewis, in the Hebrides, and southward to the Isle of Man. However, being stretched over such a large area, it was inevitable that factions would germinate and foster themselves, eventually to make claims on the leadership. Thus, on the death of one of the chiefs, a dispute arose among his followers as to his successor. There were two claimants: one was the son of the late chief, who was supported by many on that ground alone. But his character and some of his antecedents had made him so unpopular that much of his support went to the claims of a cousin, who had already proved himself to be a good soldier and a shrewd politician. Finding themselves in a minority, the cousin and his adherents returned to Uist for the purpose of laying plans for the consolidation of his claim and, *inter alia*, obtaining possession of the Isle of Skye and the important castle of Duntulm. One other important element introduced itself into the antagonism between the two cousins: they were rivals in love as well as for power. The old castle of Duntulm was the home of Margaret, an orphan and ward of the late chief, whose heart was given over to the cousin rather than to the chief's son.

After a few weeks on Uist, the cousin decided to cross the Minch, unable to bear the separation from Margaret any longer. So, on a favourable night and with only one attendant, he set sail for Skye. He reached the shore below the castle and left the attendant, to make his way slowly and cautiously up to the building. Successfully gaining entrance, he went to Margaret's room,

B

where the two young people exchanged talk about the future, a future which would always be clouded unless steps were taken to conquer the castle; so plans were laid. Margaret was to request leave to enter a convent, of which the mother superior was a relative of hers. Thus out of the way of danger, the castle was to be attacked, taken and made secure. The plan was to block every means of exit from the castle and then dig under a foundation wall, so that the building would fall by itself, burying the occupants beneath the rubble. Those that tried to escape would be caught and dealt with. The young couple talked on into the night, quite unaware the walls of the castle had ears and that every word was being heard and remembered. Later the MacDonald cousin left the castle and returned to Uist. Margaret was duly given permission to leave the castle for the convent as arranged.

The night fixed for the raid was both dark and stormy; bolts of lightning lit up the sky and ground as the raiding party landed and advanced swiftly—only to be brought up short by a dyke, which had not been there on a previous visit. Taken aback, the party had scarcely time to see the dyke begin to move before they realized that the obstruction was in reality a wall of large shields—and it was moving towards them. There was no alternative but to fight for their lives in a struggle which ended with all dead but three and the young claimant cousin taken prisoner. Before the following day had dawned, three soldiers were hanging from a gibbet in front of the castle. The young chieftain was led up to a room at the top of the castle and locked in with few furnishings save a chair, and a table on which lay a piece of salt beef, a loaf of bread and a large jug.

Hungry, though fearful of his possible fate, the lad set to and ate the bread and the beef. But the salt meat caught his throat and he reached for the jug: it was empty. As he despaired, he caught sounds from the direction of the door. At first they puzzled him; then he slowly realized that it was being blocked up.

Tradition says that years later the turret room was opened and inside was found a skeleton, grasping in its bony hands, the remains of a jug, bitten to dry dust by the thirst-maddened victim of Duntulm. As for Margaret, she waited impatiently for news of the victory. Instead, messengers arrived with the news of the crushing defeat and that her lover was a prisoner in the hands of the Laird of Duntulm. That was enough, for she knew that no mercy would be shown her if she returned to Skye. She remained in her convent and died in a few short months, to be laid to rest in the peaceful cemetery of the convent, while her lover's body slowly turned to dust in far-off Duntulm.

Despite its smallness and its remoteness from the seat of Scotland's government in Edinburgh, the island of Lewis has contributed more than its fair share to the history of the country in one way or another, but largely in connection with the need to repress unruly clans, or to intervene in clan warfare and claims for territory. The little-known 1719 'rising' was planned at Seaforth Lodge, situated just outside Stornoway, the main town on the island. And it was to Stornoway that Prince Charles Edward fled to reach the most northerly stopping place of his travels, in an attempt to obtain a ship which would take him to France and freedom, away from the English ships in the Minch and the ever-present threat of the red-coated soldiers closing in on him in the summer of the ill-fated 1746. The island traditions are full of the incidents which occurred between the various clans and families who shared out the island's land mass between them: MacAulays, Morisons and MacLeods. The MacKenzies were a later feature who appeared on the Lewis scene as the result of some rather expert double-dealing on the part of the Earl of Kintail, later to become Lord Seaforth.

The beginning of the end for the MacLeods of Lewis came when Rory MacLeod of Lewis married his third wife. The first was Barbara Stewart, daughter of Lord Methven, by whom he had a son, Torquil Oig, who died before his father, without issue. After Barbara Stewart's death, Rory took up with a daughter of the MacKenzies of Wester Ross. She bore him a son, Torquil Connaldagh, whom Rory would not acknowledge as a son, but rather held he was a bastard. The consequence of this was that Rory repudiated his wife, whom he deserted for a daughter of the powerful Clan MacLean. By this third woman he had two sons, Torquil Dow and Tormod, besides three other bastard sons, Neil,

Rory Oig, and Murdo, to the exclusion of Torquil Connaldagh. This naturally hurt the latter to the quick and he resorted to obtain what he considered his just inheritance by going to his mother's clan, the MacKenzies, and seek their help.

In a response to his request, Lord Kintail, Torquil Connaldagh and the Brieve of Lewis met to consider the situation. The Brieve of Lewis was the traditional Judge in the island; he belonged to Clan Morison of Ness, in the northern part of the island, who were enemies of the MacLeods. It was decided by the three conspirators that Lewis could not be definitely won while Torquil Dow was alive. So the Brieve undertook to trick the latter into captivity. He arranged for his galley to sail back to Ness by the remote island of North Rona, off the northern tip of Lewis. By chance, and *en route*, he fell on a Dutch ship which he pirated and decided to take what fate had given him into his plans, to trap Torquil Dow. He set sail for Stornoway, where he sent a message to old Stornoway Castle (now in ruins and under the town harbour's piles) to ask Torquil Dow to take part in a banquet to celebrate the new-found gains. Torquil, with several of his retainers, unsuspectingly went on board the ship. But instead of being given wine they were bound fast and taken to Ross, where the Lord Kintail beheaded each man of them. This occurred in July 1597.

But this effort on the part of the Brieve of Lewis did not bring the island into the hands of Torquil Connaldagh and his Mac-Kenzie relations. Instead, they found themselves opposed by Old Rory MacLeod's bastard son, Neil MacLeod, who raided Ness and killed a number of the Morisons, as reprisal for Torquil Dow's death, and he declared himself chief in possession of Lewis. The affair and its outcome left Lord Kintail pondering the question as to how to obtain Lewis for himself, having already Torquil Connaldagh as a friendly ally and also, to strengthen his position, one of Rory's sons, Tormod, whom he had kidnapped from his school. Only the intrepid Neil MacLeod stood in his way and Neil was proving himself to be no mean opponent. Kintail's first step was to persuade Torquil Connaldagh to resign all his rights to Lewis into his favour. This was done and Kintail then set to thinking about the next step to consolidate and legalize his acquisition, a step which was to be worked out for him, unknowingly, by some 'Gentlemen from Fife', known as the Fife Adventurers.

It so happened that some landed gentry from Fife had seen a report bearing on the fertility of the island of Lewis and its potential for profit. They decided the island was ripe for planning, development and exploitation as a colony, and, far down the list, in keeping with their role as speculators, 'civilizing' the island's inhabitants. They applied to and obtained from the King a gift of Lewis in 1599, which was then alleged to be at his disposal. The Fife gentlemen assembled a company of soldiers, tradesmen and others into a party which landed on the south beach at Stornoway and proceeded to build houses. They made a 'pretty' job of their new settlement, as the records stated, and were all set to consolidate themselves into a community when Neil MacLeod and his bastard brother Murdo arrived on the scene, to harry and to plunder. Many Fife heads were sent to Edinburgh in barrels of pickle as a warning to outsiders who wished to encroach on a MacLeod island.

Murdo later made the mistake of striking up friendly relations with Brieve Morison of Ness, a fact which hurt Neil, for he knew the Brieve had been instrumental in killing Torquil Dow. Eventually Murdo was taken prisoner by Neil, which event coming to the notice of the Adventurers, was followed up by a message from them to Neil to the effect that if he delivered Murdo up into their hands, Neil would be enabled to obtain a portion of Lewis for himself. This was an offer too good to miss and Neil handed over Murdo and travelled with him to Edinburgh where he was duly pardoned by the King for all his offences. Poor Murdo, on the other hand, was executed at St Andrew's, in Fife.

All this activity in Lewis had meantime prevented the Earl of Kintail from gaining some significant foothold on the island. So he set a cat among the pigeons, in the form of the kidnapped Tormod MacLeod, kept as a pawn in reserve, thinking that the arrival of the latter in Lewis would cause enough trouble for the Adventurers for him to go in and offer himself as an intermediary— though rather in his own interests than those of Tormod. This indeed is what happened, but before Kintail could capitalize on the situation, his conduct was reported to the King in Edinburgh and he was committed to ward in that city, but released soon afterwards by the intervention of the Lord Chancellor, a powerful friend in Court.

While these moves were going on, Neil had returned to Lewis and immediately fell out with his erstwhile friends, the Fife Adventurers, and resorted to his old habits of harrying their settlements at Stornoway. Tormod had, by this time, been hailed as the new chief and he joined up with Neil; both brothers then set about clearing the Adventurers from the island. But the latter, notwithstanding their burnt fingers and heels, retaliated with a strong military force the size of which made Tormod sue for a peaceful settlement and placed himself at the gentle mercy of the Adventurers. They, in their turn, delivered Tormod to the King in Edinburgh, who pardoned him but kept him ward in the city for the next sixteen years; he later died in Holland. Neil MacLeod, however, stood his ground and was such a nuisance that eventually the Adventurers became disheartened and left Lewis for the more peaceful scene in the Kingdom of Fife.

This was exactly the situation which the Earl of Kintail had waited for so long. He publicized his rights to Lewis, as assigned to him by Torquil Connaldagh. But, unexpectedly, this was not taken as having any authority in law and he was forced to resign his rights to Lewis to the King, who disposed of them to three of the more determined Fife Adventurers, who intended, come hell or high water, to mount one final attempt to colonize Lewis and turn it into a Hebridean El Dorado. They assembled a large force which landed on the island and immediately set out to hunt for Neil MacLeod. Kintail, seeing a fresh opportunity in the new development, thereupon set about to play a double game. In public knowledge he sent a supply of food and materials in a ship as aid for the Adventurers, who had found themselves scarce of victuals. At the same time he advised Neil MacLeod that should the ship not arrive at Stornoway the Adventurers would seriously think about leaving Lewis once and for all time. Neil needed no encouragement and made arrangements to intercept the ship, consolidating this move by further intensive incursions into the Adventurers' camp at Stornoway. This was the last straw and the Gentlemen from Fife indeed left Lewis for the very last time to allow the bogs, hills and moors of Lewis to settle down with no further disturbance than the occasional cry of a heron.

The titles to Lewis were then sold for a sum of money to Kintail, who became, at long last, possessor of the island. He was, however, still opposed by Neil MacLeod. Neil was eventually forced to take refuge on an island called Berisay in Loch Roag, where he kept himself and his band of followers for three years until he despaired of the situation, and wondered how he could make his peace with his King and his MacKenzie neighbours.

A solution of sorts appeared in the form of an English pirate called Peter Love or Lowe, whose ship was filled to the gunwales with great wealth pirated from trading ships intercepted in the coastal waters on the west of England and Scotland. The ship made contact with Neil MacLeod and in a short time both Love and MacLeod became fast comrades; being both rebels they had much in common. But the relationship was not to last. Capturing Love and his men, MacLeod sent them, with the pirate ship, to the Privy Council in Edinburgh, thinking that by this good deed, he would obtain his much wanted pardon. All that happened, however, was that the pirates were hanged at Leith in 1612 and Neil was forced again into hiding, this time with his cousin Sir Rory MacLeod of Harris. Neil persuaded the latter to take him to England, which Sir Rory undertook to do. But while the two were passing through Glasgow on their way south, Sir Rory was arrested and charged, under pain of treason, to deliver up Neil to the authorities, which he was finally forced to do. Poor Neil was executed in Edinburgh in April 1613, to end the MacLeod chapter in the history of the island of Lewis.

The next major incident of treachery and double-dealing in the Highlands was the massacre of Glencoe. At the time King William had become impatient with the lack of submissiveness of the Jacobite clans, chiefly MacDonalds of Glengarry, Keppoch and Glencoe, the Grants of Glenmoriston, and the Camerons of Locheil, because it caused his troops to be kept in Scotland for policing duties, which force he much wanted for his army in Flanders. His Scottish ministers, and particularly the Secretary of State, Sir John Dalrymple, Master of Stair, carried towards those clans feelings of constantly growing irritation, as latterly the principal obstacle to a settlement of the country under the new system of things. At length, in August 1691, the King issued an indemnity, promising pardon to all those who had been in arms against him before the first of the previous June, provided that they should come in at any time before the first of January the following year, and swear and sign the oath of allegiance. In essence, any chief taking the oath of allegiance to him would be allowed to develop his clan's interests.

The letters of Sir John Dalrymple from the Court at London during the remainder of the year show that he grudged these terms to the Highland Jacobites, and would have been more than happy to find that a refusal of them justified harsher measures. It was all the better that the time of grace allowed would expire in the depth of winter, for "that is the proper season to maul them, in the cold long nights".

In the middle of a letter on the subject dated 11th January (addressed to Sir Thomas Livingstone, commander in chief of the forces in Scotland), he says: "Just now my Lord Argyll tells me that Glencoe hath not taken the oaths; at which I rejoice—it's a great work of charity to be exact in rooting out that damnable sect, the worst in all the Highlands." Particular instructions subscribed by the King on the 16th, permitting terms to be offered to Glengarry, whose house was strong enough to give trouble, but adding: "If M'Ian of Glencoe and that tribe can be well separated from the rest, it will be a proper vindication of the public justice to extirpate that sect of thieves." On the same day, Dalrymple himself wrote to Colonel Hill, Governor of Inverlochy: "I shall entreat you that, for a just vengeance and public example, the thieving tribe of Glencoe be rooted out to purpose. The Earls of Argyll and Breadalbane have promised that they shall have no retreat in their bounds."

Dalrymple, however, felt that it must be "quietly done"; otherwise the clan would make shift for themselves and their cattle. There can be no doubt what he meant: merely to harry the people would make them worse thieves than before, so the MacIans had to be "rooted out and cut off".

In reality, the old Chief of Glencoe had sped to Inverlochy or Fort William before the end of the year and offered his oath to the Governor there, Colonel Hill, but, to his dismay, he discovered he had gone to the wrong officer. It was necessary, he was told, to make the journey to Inveraray, many miles distant, and there give in his submission to the Sheriff. In great and mounting anxiety, the old man toiled his way through the wintry wilderness to Inveraray. He had at one point to pass within a mile of his own house, yet he did not stop to enter it for some rest and food. After all his exertions, the old man reached Inverarary, only to find that the Sheriff absent for two days. It was not until 5th January his oath was taken and registered. The register went then to the Privy Council in Edinburgh; but the name of MacDonald of Glencoe was not found on it. It was afterwards discovered that the entry had been obliterated by some one who had taken great pains to erase it, though the entry was still traceable.

Here, then, was 'that sect of thieves' formally liable to the vengeance which the Secretary of State meditated against them. The Commander, Livingstone, wrote on 23rd January to Colonel Hamilton of the Inverlochy garrison to proceed with his work against the Glencoe clan. A detachment of the Earl of Argyll's regiment—Campbells, the hereditary enemies of the MacDonalds of Glencoe—under the command of Campbell of Glenlyon, proceeded to the glen, affecting nothing but friendly intentions, and were hospitably received. Glenlyon himself, as uncle to the wife of one of the chief's sons, was hailed as a friend.

Each morning he called at the chief's humble dwelling and took his morning draught of whisky. On the evening of the 12th he played cards with the chief's family. The final orders for the onslaught, written on 12th January, at Ballachulish, by Major Robert Duncanson (also a Campbell), were now in Glenlyon's hands: "You are to put all to the sword under seventy. You are to have a special care that the old fox and his sons do on no account escape your hands. You are to secure all avenues, that none escape; this you are to put into execution at five o'clock precisely, and by that time or very shortly after it, I'll strive to be with you with a stronger party. If I do not come to you at five, you are not to tarry for me, but to fall on."

Glenlyon was too faithful to his instructions. His soldiers had their orders the night before. John MacDonald's the chief's eldest son, observing an unusual bustle among the soldiers, took alarm, and enquired what was meant. Glenlyon soothed his fears with a story about a movement against Glengarry, and the lad went to bed. Meanwhile, efforts were being made to plant guards at the outlets from the Glen; but the deep snow which lay on the ground prevented this tactic from being fully accomplished. At five o'clock, Lieutenant Lindsay came with his men to the house of the chief; the latter, on hearing of his arrival, got out of his bed to receive him. He was shot dead as he was dressing himself. Two other people in the house shared the same fate and his wife, shamefully treated by the soldiers, died next day. Tradition says that her fingers were smashed and bitten off to get at her rings. At another hamlet in the Glen, called Auchnaion, the tacksman and his family received a volley of shot as they were sitting by their fireside, and all but one were laid dead or dying on the floor. The survivor entreated to be killed in the open air, and once outside, succeeded in making good his escape. There were similar scenes at all the other inhabited places in the glen, and before daylight, some thirty-eight persons had been murdered in cold blood. The rest of the clan, including the chief's eldest son, fled to the mountains, where many of them perished. When Colonel Hamilton came at breakfast time, he found one old man alive, mourning over the bodies of the dead; and this person, though he might have been formally exempted as being above seventy years of age, was killed on the spot. The only remaining duty of the soldiers then was to burn the houses and harry the country. This was done relentlessly and some 200 horses, 900 cattle and many sheep and goats were driven away.

A letter of Dalrymple's, dated from London, 5th March, makes us aware that the massacre of Glencoe was already making some sensation in that city. It was being said that the MacDonalds had been murdered in their beds, after the chief had made the required submission. The Secretary of State professed to have known nothing of the last fact, but he was far from regretting the bloodshed: "All I regret is that any of the sect got away." When the particulars of the deed became fully known—when it was ascertained that the Campbells had gone into the glen as friends and then fallen upon the people when they were in a defenceless state and when all suspicion was lulled asleep—the transaction assumed the character which it has born ever since in the public estimation: one of the foulest in modern history ever to be engineered by British politicians and a British king.

One very famous act of betrayal in the Highlands, though the reality of the act and its circumstances have been disputed with cogent argument, was the capture of the Marquis of Montrose by Neil MacLeod of Assynt; the deed has been remembered in the Highlands for over three hundred years in folk tradition. Highland tradition is invariably found to be closely allied to truth, only its clothing, according to the methods used for its transmission to succeeding generations, providing the difficulty in assessing its historical accuracy. In this particular case, a cloak of half-truths has tended to hide much evidence which would seem to indicate that Neil MacLeod was innocent of the charge of betrayal, in the context of traditional Highland hospitality; but he lived and died with the charge.

Recent research into the affair has, however, revealed that Neil MacLeod was unjustly accused of treachery and should now be given a clean card on the matter. In addition, evidence produced at the trial of Montrose, and subsequently, indicated that there were persuading agents in the affair, such as the 3rd Earl of Seaforth, an enemy of MacLeod, who, anxious to secure the Assynt lands for himself, went to great pains to engineer a situation where he could legally dispossess MacLeod by wrongfully accusing the latter of unpaid debts. The tradition has been carried over through the years by such writers as Bishop Wishart, Hume, Napier, John Buchan and Sir Walter Scott.

Neil MacLeod was in fact at Dunbeath in Caithness, many miles from Assynt, at the time of the alleged betrayal. This was proved in the Edinburgh courts later when Neil himself appeared on trial.

He was, it seems, in Dunbeath in his capacity as a Sheriff-Depute of Assynt to prevent any retreat of Montrose to Caithness to obtain a ship to make his escape to the Continent.

Montrose suffered the fate of any person, in despair and starving, wandering about in unfamiliar territory: lawful arrest as an enemy of the Government. Two herd boys apprehended him and brought him to Ardvreck Castle, from which a message was sent to the authorities that James Graham, Marquis of Montrose, was in their hands and secured as a prisoner. It has been alleged that Neil MacLeod's wife was in Ardvreck Castle when Montrose appeared on her doorstep. By the terms of Scottish law in those days a man was responsible for his wife's deeds, and it was not until after 1660 that such an action as 'arrest' was deemed a criminal offence. Neil's wife was the sister of Sir Andrew Munro, whose tactics led to the defeat of Montrose at Carbisdale. Thus, it would be natural for her to restrain Montrose to keep on the right side of the Government, irrespective of what the natural and common law of Highland hospitality might say about the action in such circumstances.

The Restoration in 1660 gave MacLeod's enemy, the Earl of Seaforth, the opportunity to get his hands on the Assynt estates. He approached the then Lord Advocate, also a MacKenzie, and kin to himself, and charged Neil MacLeod of betraying Montrose, thus playing a double game. MacLeod was sent for and detained in the Tolbooth, Edinburgh, for three years without being brought to trial. He protested his innocence frequently and eventually it was proved that he in fact had no personal hand in the capture of Montrose. But it was not until 1666 that King Charles II wrote a special letter to the Privy Council in Edinburgh ordering Neil MacLeod to be set free as there was no evidence upon which he could be convicted; no further proceedings were taken against MacLeod.

In the meantime, the Assynt estates and revenues were in the hands of the MacKenzies, leaving MacLeod almost a pauper. Indeed the techniques used by George, second Earl of Seaforth in 1635, to obtain, by favour of the King, the charter of the barony of the island of Lewis, was repeated by the third Earl of Seaforth to obtain the right to the superiority of Assynt. Further machinations led to Seaforth issuing MacLeod with a requirement to pay a debt of just over £200. Neil was both unable and unwilling to pay this sum, and in 1672 Seaforth obtained a commission of fire and sword against MacLeod. Assynt was ravaged as the result. For the next two decades Neil MacLeod attempted to regain his lost lands, without success, and when he died in Edinburgh in 1696, in wretched and abject poverty, he had been both the victim of cruel ill-usage and the subject of a charge of betrayal, which still stuck to his reputation in the popular mind. Only recent discoveries have cleared his name and revealed the tactics of Highland chiefs in their obsession with winning more territory to gain prestige.

In the year 1739 the people of the Outer Hebrides shivered at the news of an act of treachery which was carried out by two of their own people: the proprietors of Uist and Harris. The incident is known in Hebridean tradition as the affair of the 'Long nan Duine', the raider's ship, and is fully documented in the *Irish State Papers*, No 408.

In September, 1739, a vessel named the *William*, from Donaghadee, Ireland, with William Davidson as master, put into Loch Bracadale in Skye on the pretence of discharging some brandy there. The operation was, however, a front to conceal a discreditable plan evolved by two men: Sir Alexander MacDonald and his brother-in-law, MacLeod of Harris. Between them they had conceived the idea of deporting to the American plantations certain persons on their estates who had incurred their displeasure, and whom they described as 'thieves'. Evidence produced later, after the incident, showed that of the total number of over 100 actually deported, or kidnapped, only four or five had ever been charged with crime (sheep-stealing), and no member of the unfortunate party had ever been convicted of any crime punishable by law with death or transportation. The scheming pair employed as their agent Norman MacLeod of Bernera, Harris, who showed himself to be as unscrupulous as the means he used, as he was careful in concealing the complicity of his employers. He chartered the *William* to carry the deportees for sale to the plantations of Pennsylvania;

and he himself was to sail as supercargo and, presumably, share in the profits.

The ship was greeted with pleasure by the Skye folk when it hove to off-shore in Loch Bracadale. They expected something worthwhile from her holds. Instead, about sixty men, women and children were torn from their homes and forced down to the shore, to be bundled into the ship's holds like cattle. Before the community at large had time to shake off its numbed shock, the ship was a receding spot on the horizon, making for the west. The *William* made full sail for Finsbay, in Harris, and then went to Loch Portan, in Uist. At each of these places some twenty to thirty people received the same treatment as was meted out to the Skye folk. When the *William* finally left for Donaghadee in Ireland, 111 men, women and children were captive between decks. On the way south, the ship put five boys and girls ashore at Rum; and four adults, and the body of a young woman who died, were put on the island of Canna. Farther south, an old sick woman and two pregnant women were dumped unceremoniously on the shore on the island of Jura. All these people were marooned with no provision made for their immediate safety or sustenance; they were thought too weak to endure the journey to America.

When the *William* arrived at Donaghadee to rig and victual, the men prisoners were taken up from the hold, where they had been stowed, and the women and children from the 'tween-deck. They were all marched ashore under guard to two barns—men in one and the women and children in the other. However, though under guard, the prisoners managed to escape, to disperse throughout the Irish countryside. Many were recaptured, suffering much cruelty. The remainder were made the subject of an order subscribed to by the Irish authorities who had issued warrants for the arrest of "above ninety felons", who had "escaped" from a ship on passage "from the Highlands of Scotland to America".

But when the real facts were uncovered, that the "felons" were innocents abroad, matters changed and the authorities took the side of "the most miserable objects of compassion, and the most helpless creatures that had ever appeared to us". As the result of an official enquiry, the erstwhile captives were released unconditionally. Most of them found local employment; others managed to trace their steps to get back to their homes. No doubt there are today in County Down descendants of those Highlanders, who can trace their family origins back to the *William*.

Norman MacLeod, the agent, and his accomplice, the master of the *William*, fled the country on a warrant being issued for their arrest. The two men ultimately responsible for the affair, Mac-Donald and MacLeod, escaped punishment, though they came close to prosecution by the authorities in Edinburgh, a fate they escaped due to the fact that Duncan Forbes of Culloden used his legal knowledge and his best offices to keep his friends out of prison. It has been suggested that six years later, in 1745, when both Mac-Donald and MacLeod might have been expected to 'come out' for the Jacobites, they were found on the other side, a possible indication that Forbes of Culloden knew of their part in the *William* affair and used the fact of their complicity to keep both these gentlemen from contributing what might have been a significant element in the affairs of the Forty-five.

Highland history is but one great and complex weave. It is no surprise, therefore to find the names of Sir Alexander MacDonald and Norman MacLeod of Harris linked with the notorious kidnapping of Lady Grange, yet another piece of Highland treachery retold in Chapter Six.

Though it is the Forty-five which has captured the more permanent place in Scottish history, not to say the popular imagination, the rising of 1715 was as important historically, though equally ill-fated. As Sir Walter Scott said: "Thus ended the rebellion of 1715, without even the usual sad éclat of a defeat. It proved fatal to many ancient and illustrious families in Scotland, and appears to have been too weighty of the person whom chance or his own presumption placed at the head of it." But the Fifteen had as many consequences as had the later Forty-five. Perth, after the suppression of the rising, was made a permanent military station. A good deal of money, consequently, was circulated in the town; but the inhabitants, whatever they might have gained by the residence of the soldiers and their officers among them, were far from being fond of these guests. Squabbles often took place between them. For instance, a dancing master was killed by an officer and the circumstances of the killing made such headlines as there were in those days.

Some time in 1723, an officer of one of the regiments stationed at Perth went into a dancing school, and used indecent familiarities with a young girl. The dancing master indignantly resented the insult wantonly given to his pupil and, seizing the officer, thrust him out of the room. The officer threatened vengeance and the dancing master, nothing daunted, assured him that should they happen to meet he would find him ready. A day or two after the incident the two men met by accident; accordingly, on confronting each other, the officer and the dancing master both drew their swords. The officer, however, soon found his sword thrusts being very skilfully parried by the other who, it was said could easily have killed him. But a sergeant who attended the officer went behind the dancing master and pinned his arms back, whereupon the officer ran him through so that he died on the spot. The citizens of Perth, indignant at so foul a murder, threatened violence against the officer; but because of an interposition of the official authorities, what they had in mind for the murderer was prevented. The officer was then sent for trial and was convicted by a jury to be hanged "within three suns". His friends, however, sent an urgent message to London, applying for a pardon, which was granted. But the officer was hanged well and truly before it arrived in Perth. According to some sources, the Provost of Perth presided at the trial and the jury was composed of the city's citizens; thus the trial was hardly fair, though the sentence was justified in the eyes of common law. As a result of the officer's execution by common-law trial, an Act of Parliament was subsequently passed whereby no sentence of death or corporal punishment could take place on the south side of the River Forth in less than thirty days, or, on the north side of the river, in less than forty days. This was to ensure that pardons could be applied for and possibly granted before the execution took place. The Act was later altered so that executions could take place within three weeks after trial on the north side of the Forth, this taking account of the fact that the Highland roads and highways were being opened up to make for better communications between most parts of the region and the south.

The Battle of Culloden should have been a small entry in the history books, meriting some claim to fame as 'the last battle fought on British soil'. Certainly, if honour on the field of battle had held sway, the event might have gone down in history as simply the final episode in the short-lived Forty-five, the attempt by Prince Charles Edward Stuart to regain the Crown of the United Kingdoms for the Stuart line and dynasty. However, the cards were stacked up against Culloden being half-forgotten in such a way. Rather it stands high as a bloody peak in a range of inhuman acts of the kind which often follow total wars rather than small battles. First, Culloden presented the Government in London with the final and once-for-all opportunity to put down the Highland clans (even though not all of these were 'out' for the Stuarts) and obtain the desert which they afterwards called peace. Secondly, previous centuries of contrived strained relations between the Anglicized parts of Scotland, mainly in the lowlands, and the Gaelic-speaking parts in the Highlands, now came to a head in open warfare. One must admit here, however, that the frequent raiding forays of the Highlanders in previous times did little to endear the latter to the southerners. The fact that the Highlands were Gaelic-speaking, or had a Celtic-based linguistic background, and that they based their community life-styles and society on Celtic rhythms and logic, placed them beyond the pale of Scotland's law and Anglicized culture and were regarded as being 'barbarous', ready for any kind of civilizing influences the south cared to think up (which it later did with such agencies as the Forfeited Estates Commission and the Society in Scotland for the Propagation of Christian Knowledge).

Culloden then presented a number of opportunities to right wrongs, to settle old scores and generally to bring an area of north Britain into line with the rest of the law-abiding parts of the country. However, a more sinister element entered into the scheme of things, this being the change from the successful European general which the Duke of Cumberland was to the same person as 'Butcher Cumberland', who allowed atrocities to be committed on

F

an innocent civilian population and refused to give any quarter to those who had participated in the rising. It was the aftermath of Culloden which gave it its place in history, and which makes it today the tourists' 'must' on their Highland itinerary to the extent that more than 100,000 persons each year visit the site of the battle on the outskirts of Inverness. The after-effects of Culloden impinged on social, economic and cultural facets of the Highlands and heralded the Clearances which were to follow less than a century later and which presented scenes of echoed ferocity and examples of man's inhumanity to man.

The Highlanders on the side of the Jacobite cause were in no state to meet the well-equipped, well-fed (and indeed, wined, for the previous day had been the Duke of Cumberland's birthday, duly celebrated by his troops) military strength of the Government forces. The Highlanders had had little food, were tired from marching, were cold and wet and, possibly most significant, were uneasy for they were being required to fight on open ground. Had they retreated to their more familiar mountain ground, not two miles from Drumossie Moor, they would have been able to carry the battle for Prince Charles on for many months. As it was, the Highlanders were increasingly dispirited as the result of wrong decisions and strategic mistakes; even so, they fought bravely both as individuals and in groups. Many instances of individual heroism have been securely lodged in Highland tradition. John Mor Mac-Gilvray, major of the Mackintoshes, was at least a gun-shot past the enemy's cannons, and was surrounded by the reinforcements brought up against the Mackintoshes. He killed a dozen men with his broadsword, while some of the halberds were run into his body. When Cumberland heard of it he said he would have given a great sum of money to have saved his life. He was only one of many who gave their lives for what they thought was an honourable cause. Indeed, almost all the leaders and front-rank men of the regiments that charged the enemy sealed their devotion with their blood.

The battle lasted for only forty minutes or so, to be followed by a period of confusion and then retreat for the Highland army. No quarter was given in the pursuit. All found wearing the Highland dress, regardless of age or sex, including several of the innocent inhabitants of Inverness, whose curiosity had led them towards the scene of the fighting, were indiscriminately massacred. The course of the retreat was strewn at intervals with the slain to within a short distance of Inverness, dead bodies being found at Kingsmills and Millburn. Indeed, the retreat was more fatal than the actual engagement.

One narrator writes in *The Lyon in Mourning*: "The third day after the battle I intended to have gone the length of the field; but, on travelling little more than a mile, I was so shocked with the dismal sight I saw in that distance of the carnage made on both sides, that I returned; and pretty near Stoneyfield (on the main Inverness to Aberdeen road) I saw a beggar with his meal-pock about his neck; and at a half-mile's distance from that, a woman stripped. On my return, I came by the King's-mills and discovered some of that people, at whose doors there were twelve or fourteen corpses lying all stripped. Another woman had been killed with an infant at her breast. I saw a boy betwixt ten and twelve years of age, and his head cloven to his teeth."

Local tradition in the Highlands is both consistent and unvarying as to the accounts of the excesses committed by the English soldiery under the express orders of the Duke of Cumberland, or under such circumstances which leave the responsibility resting at his door. The topic of the cruelties perpetrated after the battle was given due treatment in a remarkable MS series of memorabilia, deposited for a number of years in the Library of the Faculty of Advocates in Edinburgh. Extending to ten volumes, suitably bound in black, with black-edged leaves, the whole was styled *The Lyon in Mourning*. The collection was formed with much pain and industry during the twenty years after Culloden by the Rev. Robert Forbes, Episcopal Minister at Leith, and latterly (titular) Bishop of Ross and Caithness, and known as Bishop Forbes. The bishop was most careful to arrive at the exact truth from his correspondents. The books confirm Highland traditional accounts of the battle and the aftermath and reveal a systematic perpetration of barbarities such as the tortures practised by the most savage Indian tribes on their victims can hardly exceed in atrocity. *The Lyon in Mourning* was printed in 1895 and reprinted in 1976.

The following are extracts from a number of writings on the
aftermath of Culloden battle; not all are from pro-Jacobite pens,
but from honest observers and interviewers who were taken aback
at the atrocities committed, even in their age where coarseness
and brutality were the order of every commoner's day:

Upon Thursday, the day after the battle, a party was ordered to
the field of battle to put to death all the wounded they should find
upon it, which accordingly they performed with the greatest despatch and the utmost exactness,—carrying the wounded from the
several parts of the field to two or three spots of rising ground,
where they ranged them in due order, and instantly shot them dead.

Upon the following day (Friday) parties were ordered to go and
search for the wounded in houses in the neighbourhood of the field,
to carry them to the field, and there to kill them.

At a small distance from the field, there was a hut for sheltering
sheep or goats in cold and stormy weather. To this hut some of the
wounded men had crawled, but were soon found out by the soldiery
who (immediately upon their discovery) made sure the door and set
fire to several parts of the hut, so that all within perished in the
flames, to the number of between thirty and forty persons, among
whom were some beggars who had been spectators of the battle in
the hopes of sharing in the plunder. Many people went and viewed
the smothered and scorched bodies among the rubbish of the hut.

(Note: The house to which this hut was attached is still to be
seen, known as Old Leanach Cottage, now a commemorative
museum and in the care of the National Trust for Scotland.)

The following description relates to the massacre of a group of
wounded Jacobite officers, taken from a vault in Culloden House;
one of the group, John Fraser, commonly called MacIver, escaped:

Some hours after the defeat of the Highland army, he (John
Fraser), with seventeen other officers of that army were carried to the
close and office houses of Culloden, where they remained for two
days, wallowing in their blood, and in great torture, without any
aid from a doctor or surgeon. The third day, Fraser and the other
seventeen wounded officers were, by a party of soldiers under the
command of a certain officer, put on carts, tied with ropes, and
carried a little distance from the house to a park dyke, when the
officer who commanded the party ordered Fraser and the other
prisoners to prepare for death; and all who were able bended their
knees and began to pray to God for mercy to their souls. In a

minute, the soldiers who conducted them were ordered to fire, which they did; and being at the distance of only two yards from the breasts of the unhappy prisoners, most of them all expired in an instant; but such was the humanity of the commanding officer, as, thinking it right to put an end to so many miserable lives, that he gave orders to the soldiers to club their muskets and dash out the brains of such of them as he observed with life, which accordingly they did; and one of the soldiers, observing John Fraser to have the signs of life after receiving a shot, he struck him on the face with the butt of his musket, broke the upper part of his nose and cheek-bone, and dashed out one of his eyes and left him for dead.

Soon after the incident, a young man, Lord Boyd, visited the scene and saw that Fraser was still living; he managed to get his servant to carry Fraser to a small corn mill on the Culloden estate, where he remained for three months enduring a slow and painful recovery. Twenty years later, Fraser, interviewed, by Bishop Forbes, was hobbling about on two crutches, visible evidence of his treatment.

When we had filled all the jails, kirks, and ships at Inverness with these rebel prisoners, wounded and naked as they were, we ordered that none should have any access to them, whether with meat or drink, for two days. By this means, no doubt, we thought at least the wounded would starve, either for want of food or clothes, the weather being then very cold. Dr Lauder's case of instruments was taken from him, for fear he should aid any of the wounded; and one John Farquharson of Aldlarg, who was, I believe, a kind of a Highland-blooder, his lancet was taken out of his pocket, for fear he should begin to blood them, to save some few of the wounded to have fallen into fevers. Some were handcuffed, especially Major Stewart and Major M'Lachlan. Their handcuffs were so tight that their hands swelled, and at last broke the skin, so that the irons could not be seen. I can compare their case to nothing better than a horse sore saddle-spoiled. In this excessive agony they were kept ten days notwithstanding all the application they made, only to get wider handcuffs, or their being changed and put upon their other hands. Among the rest I saw a Frenchman in the agonies of dying, lying in nastiness up to his stomach, and I myself put a great stone under his head, that he might not be choked, which he lay on. We always took care not to bury their dead until such time as we had at least a dozen of them. Only imagine to yourself what an unagreeable smell was there.

The following letter indicates the privations suffered by those who were sent to London in prison ships:

Gentlemen,—This comes to acquaint you that I was eight months and eight days at sea, of which time I was eight weeks upon half-a-pound and twelve ounces oatmeal, and a bottle of water in the twenty-four hours, which I was obliged to make meal-and-water in the bottom of an old bottle. There was one hundred and twenty-five put on board at Inverness, on the *James and May* of Fife. In the latter end of June, was put on board of a transport of four hundred and fifty ton, called the *Liberty and Property*, in which we continued the rest of the eight months, upon twelve ounces of oat sheeling as it came from the mill.

There was thirty-two prisoners more put on board the said *Liberty and Property*, which makes one hundred and fifty-seven; and before we came ashore there was only life in forty-nine, which would have been no great surprise if there had not been one, conform to our usage. They would take us from the hold in a rope, and hoisted us up to the yardarm, and then let us fall into the sea, in order for ducking of us; and tying us to the mast and whipping us if we did anything however innocent that offended them: this was done to us when we was not able to stand. I will leave it to the readers to judge what condition they might be in themselves with the above treatment. We had neither bed nor bed-clothes, nor clothes to keep us warm in the day-time. The ship's ballast was black earth and small stones, which we was obliged to dig holes to lie in to keep us warm, till the first of November last, that every man got about three yards of gross harn filled up with straw, but no bed-clothes. I will not trouble you more till I see you . . . I am, gentlemen, your most humble servant, (signed) Will Jack, Tilbury Fort, March 17th, 1747.

On shore, Highlanders who found themselves in prisons fared no better:

. . . After we brought them up the river Thames, we got orders to separate their officers from what they called soldiers, and bring the officers to Southwark New Jail, and leave the commons at Tilbury Fort, without meat, drink, money, or clothes; and actually they would have starved, had it not been for the charity of the English, the government not giving them one sol to live upon, except those few that turned evidence; it's no great wonder if they had all turned evidence to get out of this miserable situation, the prospect of which behoved to appear worse than death, for, in my opinion, nothing could come up to it, save the notion we conceive of hell; and

I do not know if hell itself be so bad, only that it may be of a longer duration. But to return to our gentlemen officers: they were brought up in rank and file, exposed to the fury of a tumultous mob who neither spared them with their outrageous words, spittles, dirt, and even stones and bricks, and in that manner carried through all the streets in Southwark, and at last delivered over to the hands of a jailer, who neither had the least fear of God, nor humanity,—a creature entirely after their own heart, who loaded them, the moment they entered his gates, with heavy irons and bad usage.

After every execution, the mangled bodies were brought back to the jail, and remained there some days, to show the remaining prisoners how they were to be used in their turn. I am very sure nothing could be more shocking to nature than to see their comrades, their friends, brought back in such a condition, all cut to pieces—the very comrades they parted with an hour-and-a-half before in perfect good health and top spirits. They had even the cruelty to keep the reprieves of those that were to be saved till some hours before their execution.

The Duke of Cumberland himself was not quite free from guilt in the Culloden affair. On his command, some sixty-nine men from Glenmoriston and twelve from Glenurquhart, induced by the Laird of Grant to come to Inverness to surrender, were made prisoners and put on board ship; such as did not die there were sent to Barbados, where, three years after, only eighteen of the whole number were still surviving. ·

Once it became known that prisoners of war were being killed by starvation, neglect of wounds, hypothermia and other means, a number of English notables, to their lasting credit, took it upon themselves to investigate the situation, though too late to obtain the reprieve of many prisoners; these included Lord Mahon and Tobias Smollett, and such organs as the *Anti-Jacobin Review*. Smollett records:

> In the month of May the Duke of Cumberland advanced with the army into the Highlands, as far as Fort Augustus, where he en-camped, and sent off detachments on all hands to hunt down the fugitives, and lay waste the country with fire and sword. The castles of Glengarry and Lochiel were plundered and burned; every house, hut or habitation met with the same fate without distinc-tion; all the cattle and provisions were carried off; the men were either shot upon the mountains like wild beasts, or put to death in

cold blood, without form of trial; the women, after having seen their husbands and fathers murdered, were subjected to brutal violation, and then turned out naked, with their children, to starve on the barren heaths. The ministers of vengeance were so alert in the execution of their office, that in a few days there was neither house, cottage, man, nor beast, to be seen in the compass of fifty miles— all was ruin, silence, and desolation.

The royal army also amused itself by burning or otherwise destroying all that came within its reach on some of the Highland estates. Among the rest, Beaufort Castle and all the buildings of the Lovat Estates were reduced to ashes. In Glenstrathfarrar, everything was destroyed, though before burning the dwellings of the folk there, they were ransacked by soldiers who looted any valuables they found. One military party was highly pleased with their work and, after sorting articles of value, loaded them onto a white horse which, in the company of two soldiers, was sent on to a place of safety. However, the small party was met by two Glenstrathfarrar men, still smarting under the destruction of their homes. Challenging the soldiers, they fell on them and killed one; the second managed to escape with his life to the military camp at Raonfearna, at Struy.

The Glenstrathfarrar men, however, were less in possession of their senses than befitted Highlanders. The white horse was stripped of its load of valuables and a dirk thrust into each side of its heart. A pit was dug and the horse buried alongside the murdered soldier. They then made off into the hills. Meanwhile, the soldier who had escaped told his tale to his commanding officer, and in no time every soldier and officer in the district was determined to retaliate in some way to avenge the death of their comrade in arms. When the news of the deed reached Major Lockhart in Inverness, he immediately ordered certain companies to be made ready to burn the country of The Chisholm in Strathglass; to ram home his intentions to keep order by force, he selected two officers for the expeditions, who were John and James Chisholm, sons of The Chisholm. This selection was considered both harsh and cruel, even in military circles. Pleading to be released from their commission, the Chisholm brothers found no pity in Lockhart's heart or mind and they were dismissed from his presence. Later that night a stray bullet somehow found its home in the major's body and he died; thus Fate intervened to release the sons from their dreadful commission and Strathglass was saved from fire and sword. This major had an evil reputation. Once he had marched with a detachment into the lands of the MacDonalds of Barisdale and burnt the houses. Some of the people had in fact a paper of protection signed by Lord Loudon; but the Major paid them no attention and replied that not even a warrant from Heaven would make him disregard what he thought was his proper duty.

A tradition in Glencannich tells of the brutal murder of a child. This occurred in the village of Tombuie. The village folk were out shearing corn when the redcoats appeared. Feared for their lives they fled for safety. One woman, however, became frantic when she remembered that her child had been left asleep in the house. From the distance, the folk could see the soldiers going around the houses and one in particular going into the woman's house. It afterwards transpired that this soldier had gone into the house and drawn his sword from its scabbard. But the sunlight caught on the metal which shone with such brilliance that the child laughed and clapped its hands at the sight. The would-be executioner stayed his hand and hesitated between his orders to put all to the sword and the dictates of conscience and humanity. He sheathed his sword and turned to go outside. There he was met by a comrade who asked if he had found anyone inside. He received an answer in the negative, but, being suspicious, went in to check and emerged with the mangled body of the infant transfixed on his sword.

Lochaber, a district particularly inhabited by staunch Jacobites, came under the fire and attention of the Royalist troops and bore the full brunt of the merciless punishment. Innocents were slaughtered when they had no case to answer for. One day news was sent to Mrs Cameron of Glen Nevis House that the redcoats were in the neighbourhood, wreaking vengeance and that the house was on their list for searching. With great presence of mind she gathered all the silverplate and other valuables, wrapped them in blankets and buried them deep in an outside garden wall. She then took herself and her children, with a few personal maids, to a cave far up the glen. The soldiers were naturally upset at finding the house already stripped of its valuables and in revenge wreaked more havoc among the folk of the glen by killing and burning.

They located Mrs Cameron's hideout and insisted that she leave with them but she refused. One soldier noticed that she had something bulky beneath her dress which she guarded carefully. Thinking it might be something of value, he slit open the dress to find nothing more than her infant son only a few months old. The knife blade went into his neck but he was not seriously wounded. Eventually he became Laird of Glen Nevis and until his dying day he bore the mark of the wound. The soldiers went off content with silver buttons and gold lace cut from the garments of the captives.

It is pleasant to make a change from treachery to cite the instance of Roderick MacKenzie, proving that honour existed side by side with what has been written above. His act was one of self-sacrifice, and it is commemorated in the grave and cairn which can be seen near Ceann–na–Cnoc, in Glenmoriston, Inverness-shire. MacKenzie was an officer in the Jacobite Army at the time of the Forty-five. In many ways he closely resembled the Prince in appearance, a fact which fate decided would at once be the death of him, but would also give him an honoured place in history and in the long-standing Highland folk memory.

After Culloden he, like many others, managed to escape and went into hiding, in his case, in Glenmoriston. He lay low for some time then, after hearing rumours that the redcoats were searching in the district for the Prince who, it was also rumoured was in the district on his way to the west coast, he emerged from his hiding place and came out into open ground. It was not long before he was seen and, because of his resemblance to the Prince, hotly pursued. He was overtaken at Ceann–na–Cnoc, but turned on his pursuers. He fought hard and bravely but was overwhelmed. At last, dying on his feet from multiple wounds, he fell to the ground crying: "Alas, you have slain your Prince!"

The troops who had both chased and killed him were highly excited, though it is said that some of them expressed fears of the consequences of killing royalty. In the event, they cut off Mac-

Kenzie's head, buried his body where it lay and made post haste for Fort Augustus. There was no one at the fort who could readily identify the head, nor who could, even from memory, swear to it that the Prince was indeed now dead and headless. So the gruesome relic was put into a tub of pickle and sent south. In the meantime, while confirmation was awaited, the search for the real Prince was slackened off, a fact which undoubtedly gave the latter some much-need respite. Indeed, in some districts the searching forays were called off altogether. By the time it was confirmed that the head sent south was not even remotely royal, the Prince had escaped to France and to safety.

MacKenzie's act was not forgotten and a cairn was raised over the spot where his headless body was buried. It seems strange that this act of selfless heroism, admittedly one among many others, has never received some merited recognition in either Jacobite poetry or song, popular or otherwise.

What is popularly known as the Clearances lasted continuously in the Highlands and Islands of Scotland from before the Forty-five until the latter end of the nineteenth century. This particular period of Highland history was, in its many aspects, no worse in terms of inhumanity, barbarity, and insensitivity, than in periods in the region's previous history; but what made it a particularly bitter experience was that the hundred years or so of activity involved in clearing people off the land, to which they had assumed they had some kind of inalienable right of possession, saw a number of variations on the theme of treachery. Often impinging on personal loyalties, one variety of treachery compounded another and served only to create an isolation and dreadful polarization between those being cleared and those implementing policies which, however well-meaning in their blissful planning, meant death, tragedy and often despair at the conduct of honourable institutions such as the established Church.

On the one hand the treachery was actively played out by the Government, the Church, the erstwhile clan chiefs, the Scottish legal system, and the aspiring system of the early Victorian era in which honours were heaped upon those who had amassed fortunes off the backs of those unfortunates who were compelled to leave their rural environment for a crammed and cramped urbanized and industrialized life of grinding poverty. On the other hand, the victims of the Clearances were often simple folk, sure about one single thing in their subsistence-based lives: that they, as members of their clan, had an inalienable right to the land which they, and their forebears before them, had tilled and brought into a fruitfulness which, while adding little to the gross national product, at least saved them from being a chargeable burden on the State.

The Highland Clearances have excited such an extent of interest and literary outpourings that they run a close second to the Forty-five, and, which might be expected, has evoked opinions from persons as wide apart as Napoleon and Karl Marx. Indeed, the latter's comments on the Clearances make one wonder that the rise in British politics of the Gael and crofters in later years of the nineteenth century, during which the Crofters Act was passed in 1886, did not take a greater lurch to the Socialist left to produce a hardened Communist faction in the Highlands. Perhaps the fact that Gaelic-based Celtic society is already inherently communalistic in its nature and structure, and was not based solely on hard materialism, prevented the Highlands and Islands from producing the revolutionary elements which so disrupted French society in the eighteenth century and Russian society in the early parts of the present century.

The rôle of the Government was a base one. After the Forty-five the Government manœuvred the martial Highlanders into accepting employment in the Army of the day. Highlanders in Highland regiments, often commanded by their chief, or his near relations, fought battles all over the world, particularly in India and the Far East where massive commercial operations required their services to maintain the flow of profits of such empires as the East India Company. During the war against the French Revolution and Napoleon, the Isle of Skye alone furnished thousands of men for the forces. By 1837 Skye alone had contributed to the British Army twenty-one Lieutenant-Generals and Major-Generals, forty-eight Lieutenant-Colonels, 600 Majors, Captains and Subalterns, 120 pipers and 10,000 non-commissioned officers and men. Men from Sutherland fought under Gustavus Adolphus, and had become the fame of the armies in Europe. Many men fought in the British Army merely on the promise made by the authorities that they and their families would get some plot of land to call their own. But when the fighting was finished and Highlanders made their way back to their home villages, they found nothing but blackened ruins, and their families scattered over the moors, if not already on their enforced way to the Americas, embarked on 'coffin ships'. Thus, when the Crimean War was occupying the attention of the authorities in London, of thirty-three infantry battalions sent to the Crimea, only three were Highland: the 42nd, the 79th and the 93rd. By the autumn of 1854, when Sir Colin Campbell's Highland Brigade at Balaclava consisted only of the 93rd Sutherland Highlanders, the question was asked: Where are the Highlanders? What the Press, the pulpit, Parliament, and those in cosy withdrawing-rooms in the laird's Highland seats had forgotten was that there were few Highlanders left. What was not considered was the simple fact that districts which had previously yielded thousands of young soldiers were now empty except for shepherds and sheep. The Sutherland parishes of Farr and Kildonan which had supplied most of the men for the famous 93rd regiment could, in 1854, scarcely muster a company of men. The glens of Ross-shire were similarly deserted. The 79th regiment could never again replace lost blood with Camerons from Lochaber. Another unconsidered fact was that in the past the chiefs had raised their regiments as much by threat of eviction as by appeals to the loyalties of their clansmen.

Thus, in 1854, the Highlanders were disinclined to turn out to fight the Russians. In that same year occurred one of the many similar scenes in the Highlands, described by John Prebble in his *The Highland Clearances*:

> Four miles down the glen, as they came through a wood by the march of Greenyard, their road was blocked by sixty or seventy women, with a dozen or less men standing behind them. The women had drawn their red shawls over their heads, and were waiting silently. Taylor, the Fiscal, and Stewart, got down from the carriage and walked to the head of the police. Taylor shouted to the women in Gaelic and told them that they must clear the way for the Law, and when they did not move he took out the Riot Act and began to read it. . . . The constables went forward with their truncheons

lifted, and, according to the *Inverness Courier* (which got its information from Taylor) the Strathcarron men immediately ran for the hills, leaving their women alone. Although some men must have remained, for two were injured and one was later charged, the absence of all the others is hard to condone, as it was at Culrain, Gruids, and elsewhere. The assault of the police was short, brutal and bloody. The *Courier*, again reporting Taylor perhaps, said that there were three hundred women there, and that they were armed with sticks and stones. If they were, they were remarkably inefficient in the use of them for no policeman suffered more than a bruise or a dented hat. . . .

Five years previously, at Sollas, North Uist, Archibald Dubh Macdonnell, threatened with eviction, called up his seven stalwart sons, armed himself with a broadsword his grandfather had carried at Culloden, and defied both the Law and his chief.

It was at the behest of lairds and landlords that the Government authorized the despatch of gunboats and armed militia to quell demonstrations by crofters armed with sticks and stones.

When the deaf, old and infirm Duke of Sutherland travelled north from London to encourage his tenants to enlist in the British Army, he called a meeting of all the male inhabitants of Clyne, Rogart and Golspie. Not all heeded the call, but 400 turned up to pay him his due as a laird. He spoke from a table piled high with notes and coins and explained the necessity of going to war with the Russian Czar who was ruling with all the power of a tyrant and despot. Queen Victoria desperately needed their support. After he finished he sat down and there ensued an awkward silence at which he became indignant and asked for an explanation. One old man stood up and said: "I am sorry for the response your Grace's proposals are meeting here, but there is a cause for it . . . It is the opinion of this county that should the Czar of Russia take possession of Dunrobin Castle and of Stafford House next term that we couldn't expect worse treatment at his hands than we have experienced at the hands of your family for the last fifty years . . . How could you expect to find men where they are not, and the few of them which are to be found among the rubbish or ruins of the country have more sense than to be decoyed by chaff to the field of slaughter. But one comfort you have. Though you cannot find men to fight, you can supply those who will fight with plenty of mutton, venison and beef."

In the event, only one man joined up and took the Duke's offer. But no sooner had he arrived at Fort George, near Inverness, than his house was pulled down, his wife and family turned out and only permitted to live in a hut from which an old female pauper was carried away a few days before to the churchyard.

Some men, disbanded from the famous 93rd at Balaclava, with the sounds of battle still resounding in their ears, returned home to their Parish of Lairg to find that a factor, known as Domhnall Sgrios, Donald Destruction, had beaten them to it and had cleared all their families and pulled their houses down. The thought of fighting for queen and country in remote Balaclava might have raised their morale and spirits, but their efforts did not give them the land on which they could live in peace with their families.

The legal system of Scotland largely displayed its professionalism by acting more on behalf of those who had the wherewithal to pay fat fees for drawing up instruments with which the folk were cleared off the land. The prime example of betrayal by the legal fraternity was seen at the trial of Patrick Sellar in Inverness in 1816. There was a jury of fifteen men, eight of whom were local landed proprietors, two were merchants, two were tacksmen, one a lawyer and the rest magistrates and justices of peace. All were mature enough in years to have memories of the clearances. Sellar was charged with "culpable homicide, as also oppression and real injury" and with "wickedly and maliciously setting on fire and burning", charges which could be proved. The charge against Sellar was so long that it took nearly two hours to read it to the court. The jury took only fifteen minutes to declare Sellar innocent of all charges; it was congratulated by the Judge for its decision. Later, with the stamp of legal approval on all his deeds, Sellar continued his evictions, though with more subtleties as to his tactics.

The Church, too, must take its share of the charge of treachery and betrayal of the very people it should have protected. The Ministers of the Established Church, in particular, but with a few notable exceptions, did nothing to prevent the atrocities and inhumanities which often took place within sight of the manse door.

The record of the Free Church of Scotland is better than that of the Established Church. The people were persuaded, dishonestly, that their troubles were the result of God's punishment for being a sinful people. When the people of Glencalvie were evicted (May 1845), they sought refuge in Croick churchyard and they scratched a few messages for posterity on the window-pane. The most pathetic, and in many ways the most revealing, reads: "Glencalvie people the wicked generation." Ministers thundered from their pulpits that the evictions were 'the judgment of God'; the effect was to induce into the minds of their flocks a hopeless apathetic subjection which sapped their will to resist their oppressors.

Clan chiefs were no less innocent of the charge. Some chiefs pursued the clearing of their clansmen with a zeal born of the ultimate in alienation from culture, language and kinship; the result of their galloping anglicization and the gradual erosion of their old patriarchal status in the eyes of their clansmen. Their contribution to the social engineering methods of the Highlands for the benefit of the wealthy capitalist was considerable and, because of their quasi-association with their territory, the more abominable.

To instance only a few of the incidents which occurred during the height of the Clearances is to offer for viewing a small corner of a terrifying picture of cruelty perpetrated on a submissive people who were as bewildered as to the causes for change in their station as were the sheep which were later to replace them when chased by dogs.

Donald MacLeod, who witnessed many of the Sutherland evictions, later wrote a book called *Gloomy Memories*, in which he related the history of the Clearances. The title was in reply to *Sunny Memories* written by Harriet Beecher Stowe (author of *Uncle Tom's Cabin*), who was persuaded to whitewash the Duke of Sutherland's ultimate responsibility for the terrible hardships his clearances produced. MacLeod wrote:

> The cries of the victims, the confusion, the despair and horror painted on the countenances of the one party, and the exulting ferocity of the other, beggar all description. In these scenes Mr Sellar was present, and apparently, as sworn by several witnesses at his subsequent trial, ordering and directing the whole. Many deaths

ensued from alarm, from fatigue, and cold, the people having been instantly deprived of shelter and left to the mercies of the elements. Some old men took to the woods and to the rocks, wandering about in a state approaching to, or of absolute insanity; and several of them in this situation lived only a few days. Pregnant women were taken in premature labour, and several children did not long survive their sufferings. To these scenes I was an eye-witness, and am ready to substantiate the truth of my statements, not only by my own testimony, but by that of many others who were present at the time. In such a scale of general devastation, it is almost useless to particularize the cases of individuals; the suffering was great and universal. I shall, however, notice a very few of the extreme cases of which I myself was an eye-witness. John MacKay's wife, Ravigill, in attempting to pull down her house, in the absence of her husband, to preserve the timber, fell through the roof. She was in consequence taken in premature labour, and in that state was exposed to the open air and to the view of all the bystanders. Donald Munro, Garvott, lying in a fever, was turned out of his house and exposed to the elements. Donald MacBeath, an infirm and bed-ridden old man, had the house unroofed over him, and was in that state exposed to the wind and rain until death put a period to his sufferings. I was present at the pulling down and burning of the house of William Chisholm, Badinloskin, in which was lying his wife's mother, an old bed-ridden woman of nearly one hundred years of age, none of the family being present. I informed the persons about to set fire to the house of the circumstances, and prevailed on them to wait until Mr Sellar came. On his arrival, I told him of the poor woman being in a condition unfit for removal, when he replied: "Damn her, the old witch, she has lived too long—let her burn." Fire was immediately set to the house, and the blankets in which she was carried out were in flames before she could be got out. She was placed in a little shed, and it was with great difficulty they were prevented from firing it also. . . . Within five days she was a corpse.

In the Parish of Kildonan, some 2,000 people were forcibly removed from their homes, which were burnt out in a conflagration which lasted nearly a week to produce a scene of warlike devastation. So thick was the smoke blowing off-shore that one fishing boat lost its way and could only make off to sea at nightfall, when she found her bearings by the light of the flames inland. One man, Donald MacKay, carried two of his children, both of whom were suffering from fever, a distance of twenty-five miles to a ship at Caithness. Steps were taken to prevent those made homeless from scraping up shellfish at Little Ferry, by the posting there of police constables.

There were clearances in many other parts of the Highlands and Islands, but the Sutherland Clearances are an unenviable highlight in a period of Highland history which has earned for itself a place in the long-standing memory of the folk, attended by a large corpus of songs and poetry in Gaelic which is sung and recited at *ceilidhs* today with as much feeling as though the events had taken place but yesterday.

FOUR

Beyond the Law

Living beyond the law in the Scottish Highlands has a number of meanings. In the first instance, the 'law' was often an arbitrary decision by a chief to place a person out of the benefits of common protection, and often for an ulterior motive. Then came 'law' generated from political considerations which placed not only individuals but whole communities or clans at risk from any person or body in the remaining 'protected' community hoping to gain by seeking out and arresting or killing. Commissions of 'fire and sword' were often obtained by the unscrupulous against neighbours on false charges, by which means the former hoped to get their hands on the possessions, titles and financial benefits of the latter. Others found themselves outside the pale of the law because of their crimes committed against others, and these were justly rewarded situations. In this chapter is presented an interesting kaleidoscope of individuals and groups who have added interest if not lustre to Highland history and serve to underline the fact that they were the exceptions rather than the rule—and, indeed, that life was never based on a solid foundation of surety, but was ever subject to whims of both individuals and governments.

About the middle of the sixteenth century a fierce family feud began between the Grant Houses of Carron and Ballindalloch, which is typical of the 'good old days of yore'. An attempt had been made by Grant of Ballindalloch to deprive young Patrick Grant, of Glenmoriston, of his rights to the Glenmoriston inheritance. Patrick's natural brother, John Roy Grant of Carron, interfered to support the boy's rights. In an ensuing quarrel Grant of Ballindalloch was killed. Time passed and should have healed wounds; in this case, however, time served rather to simmer feelings until they reached boiling point nearly a century later. In the year 1615 a son of Grant of Carron, attending a Fair at Elgin, was savagely attacked by one of the Ballindalloch Grants. James Grant, another member of the Carron family, who was present, immediately set upon his brother's assailant and killed him outright. James was in due course summoned to appear at Court on a charge of murder; but he refused to submit and was declared an outlaw.

Accompanied by a small band of desperate characters, James took refuge in the wilds of western Strathspey, making himself and his followers notoriously troublesome and disagreeable to many families in the surrounding districts. He also paid particular attention, with great intent and purpose, to the House of Ballindalloch. Soon James Grant became known as Seumas an Tuim— James of the Knoll—popular in local tale and legend.

But James and his band often overstepped the mark and many innocent and poor people had cause to lose the original sympathy which he had won from them when he was unjustly outlawed. However, despite complaints to the authorities, who were in any case few and far between, they could do little to curb the raids on their properties. In time, power was given to the Laird of Grant to bring James the freebooter to book at any cost. Though the sum of 5,000 Scots merks was offered as a reward for his apprehension, the outlaw was not easily caught. But one man in particular was anxious to settle old scores; James Grant of Ballindalloch expressed often his keenness to capture James the Outlaw, to deprive the latter of both liberty and life. So he plotted to find some way to bring the outlaw into the open. The plan he eventually carried out was the cruel killing of John Grant of Carron, and some of his people, when they were in the Forest of Abernethy cutting timber. Though Ballindalloch lost some of his own men in this skirmish, he was well satisfied that James the Outlaw would appear for revenge and fall into his hands. James did in fact appear, but only to visit Ballindalloch's properties to burn them to the ground with all stock, cattle, corn, goods and gear; and he escaped.

Matters came to a head shortly afterwards and the Earl of Moray, determined for some peace in the lands under his jurisdiction, took the affair into his own hands, by laying a trap which resulted in the capture of the outlaw in his own house in Strathaven. The incident lost James some of his men and he himself sustained some wounds. But captured he was and, after a period of recovery, he was sent to be imprisoned in Edinburgh Castle. There he was a prisoner for two years until he escaped, with the help of his wife who, on a visit, brought in a rope hidden in a small cask of butter. That night in the autumn of 1632, James of the Knoll was back in his old haunts in the Highlands once more.

A large reward for his re-apprehension was offered by the Privy Council in Edinburgh, but there were no claimants. Ballindalloch still remained as eager as ever to bait James but, though a few minor incidents occurred, the outlaw kept himself out of harm's way until, towards the end of his life, he was given a full pardon— for he had in fact gone to the aid of his brother when he was attacked at the Elgin Fair, and killed in self-defence. He died a natural death calmly and in his own bed in 1639. There are a number of caves in Strathaven traditionally associated with the outlaw as his hiding places. On the eastern side of Loch Ness, between Foyers and Dores, there are caves in which the outlaw is said to have taken refuge. He was generally popular, despite his trade, and there were not a few who admired the freedom and the romance of his enforced profession. In a Gaelic song, of which James of the Knoll was the subject, the composer writes:

> My love o'er all men is to James of the Knoll;
> You would run and jump and so neatly dance;
> You would wrestle strong men off their feet;
> And your courage never failed,
> Nor your cleverness and resources.

In the year 1649 an outlaw cateran named MacAllister, with a large band of eager followers, kept a large portion of Caithness in terror. The people of Thurso having, to his mind, somehow given him offence, he decided to revenge himself by suddenly coming down upon them on a Sunday and burning them in church. He and his men provided themselves with withies of twigs to fasten the doors, in order to keep the people shut in, while the building was set on fire. Someone remonstrated with him for contemplating such an unholy design on the Sabbath-day, but he avowed that, in spite of both God and the Sabbath, he would shed blood. Fortunately, some humane person became aware of the plan and set off in front of the raiding party to give the alarm. This had scarcely been done when MacAllister and his men arrived; some twenty in number they presented a fearsome crowd. There were seven doors in the church, as may be verified by an inspection of the ruins to this day. An old woman dexterously thrust her stool into one near which she sat, so as to prevent it from being closed; the people inside were more than keen to defend the rest as best they could.

MacAllister himself came to the door of the gallery at the southwest angle of the building. But here sat Sir James Sinclair of Murkle, an able and determined man who made a practice of coming to church armed. Meeting the robber in the doorway, he thrust his sword through him, but with no apparent effect. Sir James' servant, however, superstitiously fearing that MacAllister was impervious to cold steel, cut a triangular button from Sir James' coat and, with that makeshift bullet, shot MacAllister in the head. He tumbled over the stair with a mortal wound in the ear. The rest of the raider party were then set upon by the congregation and, after a hard contest, overpowered many of them and killed not a few, leaving local legend to form its own morals about the business of desecrating the Sabbath.

Among the hills of Rangag, Latheron, in Caithness, beside where the Causewaymire road winds its way through the moors from Latheron to Georgemas, lies Loch Rangag. A few hundred years ago this area was a forbidden land and any person who ventured into it was lucky to escape with his life. On a small peninsula by the side of the loch are the ruins of a small castle or keep. In this castle in the early seventeenth century lived a notorious robber and freebooter by the name of Greysteel. His dates are in some doubt, varying from the thirteenth century; but it appears that he flourished around the late sixteenth and early seventeenth century. Tradition does not give us his real name, but his nickname, Greysteel, is sufficient to point to his character, a man of powerful build and great strength. His ability with the sword was well known and no man could engage him in conflict and live to tell the tale.

Some local folk believed him to be a disciple of the Devil charged with wreaking vengeance on the people of Caithness for their religious views. Many stories are told of Rob Roy and other outlaws who exercised kindness and mercies towards their enemies. But Greysteel was different; often he would stop short of killing an opponent, mortally wounded, just for the pleasure of seeing him die slowly and in great pain. He ravaged the countryside, waylaid travellers and made frequent raiding excursions into Sutherland. Altogether he was a bad stick; but Fate was preparing his destiny.

One day a young son of Sinclair of Rattar accidentally strayed onto Greysteel's land. Word was sent to the outlaw that a man was hunting near the west end of Loch Rangag and he immediately set out to challenge the intruder. Young Sinclair was no match for the robber and he received a fatal stroke from Greysteel's sword. The body was stripped of its valuables and thrown into the loch. In time young Sinclair's family was told of the death and they grieved in gloom, along with the dead man's friend, another Sinclair, the Laird of Dunn, at Watten.

He swore to take revenge for his friend's death and stated his intention to go to Loch Rangag and challenge Greysteel to a duel. Though he was advised not to be so rash, he persisted in his stated intention and for days brooded on the matter. Then one morning at an early hour he rose and stole away from his family's house equipped with his best sword and shield and made for Loch Rangag. But he got caught up in a storm and had to make for the shelter of a cottage. It was occupied by an old woman who offered him a bed for the night and a share in her little store of poor food. As he ate, Dunn noticed a very unusual-looking sword standing in a far corner. He was greatly struck by its appearance. The hilt was covered with a variety of jewels and strange carvings which seemed to indicate a foreign origin. He asked the old woman about it and was told that the sword belonged to her late husband who was a William MacKay and a sergeant in Lord Reay's Regiment. He fought in Germany and was for a time in the service of King Gustavus Adolphus of Sweden. Her husband came on the sword in a town called Frankfurt-on-Oder. One day he witnessed a Polish

Jew being attacked by a set of ruffians and he went to his aid. Grateful, the Jew presented MacKay with the sword which was supposed to be endowed with wonderful properties, so that any who fought with it in battle would win over an opponent. The sword was now a family heirloom and could never be the property of another. But young Sinclair was determined at least to have the use of the weapon and he told her of his mission and asked her if he could borrow the sword for a day, until he had finished Grey-steel. The old woman took a lot of persuasive talking until she relented and the sword was handed over.

The next morning, after the weather had cleared, Greysteel's watchmen reported a man making towards Loch Rangag. The outlaw, keen for a new victim of his skill, set off to meet the intruder. The two opponents soon met and battle commenced. Greysteel used all his knowledge to seek out a weakness in his challenger but could find none. The strange sword in the young man's hand seemed to be everywhere to parry each thrust he made.

The struggle was bitter and unrelenting, each man being a match for the other, with young Sinclair amazed at the dexterity he suddenly found in his sword-arm. In time Greysteel began to tire and in one last attempt to kill the young man he lunged, but his sword was parried. The movement threw Greysteel off his balance and, quick as lightning, young Sinclair thrust his sword through the robber's heart. With a great roar that echoed through the hills, Greysteel, the terror of Caithness, threw his hands in the air in disbelief and fell dead on the heather. The robber's retainers, watching the fight from the castle, were amazed that their leader had succumbed to a young stripling. The victor, in haste, left the scene of the killing and returned with a band of willing followers who set to raze the castle to the ground, killing many of the robber band. The wonderful sword was then handed back to the old woman, who was given in reward a new cottage near Dunn rent-free for the rest of her life.

It was noted in 1676 that a 'remarkable homicide' took place in the village of Aberfeldy in Perthshire. A butcher and another man sitting in an ale-house began to quarrel and, in a sudden fit of passion, the butcher inflicted a mortal stab upon his companion.

Some gentlemen, sitting in the next room, heard the commotion and, rushing in, found the butcher with the bloody knife in his hand. Excited by the atrocity of the deed, they hurried off the murderer to the regality gallows and instantly hanged him, though they had no sort of authority to act in that manner. They probably acted on a popular notion that a murderer, taken red-handed or fresh from the act of killing, may be instantly done to death by the bystanders.

One day in May 1752, Colin Campbell, the red-haired proprietor of Glenure, a small estate in the North Lorne area of Argyll, became the victim of what is now known as the 'Appin Murder'. It stands in the same rank and standing as a number of famous trials of world-wide fame, for an innocent man was hanged for the crime and the trial still occupies legal minds today who give the verdict that it was a particularly nasty piece of Highland history and was a travesty of justice which placed an innocent man beyond the law and its protection, to satisfy ulterior motives. There are, it is said, some persons living today who know the name of the true murderer, but who are sworn to secrecy and can only pass the name from one generation to another under some terrible oath. Robert Stevenson used the incident of the murder in his novels *Kidnapped* and *Catriona*; unfortunately Stevenson allowed his aim at telling a good story to get in the way of history; many later recounters of the murder have used Stevenson as their starting point rather than the older traditional accounts which exist including one at least, in the Gaelic language.

Stevenson wrote: "This is no furniture for the scholar's library, but a book for the winter evening school-room when the tasks are over and the hour for bed draws near." The hero of Stevenson's books is David Balfour, who never figured in anything connected with the Appin Murder. Stevenson also invented a military escort for Colin Campbell of Glenure, a device which provided for a spirited chase over the hills after the killing. The fixed point on which the story pivots is September 1752, some four months after the murder was committed. This period, however, was long enough for Stevenson to allow for all the perils that were to befall David Balfour, as recounted in the pages of *Catriona*. Even so, despite

Stevenson's many departures, some quite serious from the view-
point of the historian, he has helped considerably in maintaining
interest in an incident which has justifiably caught and held the
public's imagination. Inevitably, many traditions have grown up
around the murder, the trial, and the subsequent hanging of James
Stewart, the unfortunate innocent, whose memory has long been
revered by Highlanders, both sympathetic and partisan.

The victim, Colin Campbell of Glenure, served in the Forty-five
with a commission in Lord Louden's Regiment. During the early
days of the rising, Glenure was actively engaged in patrol and re-
connaissance duties on the bleak moor of Rannoch. His command
included a party of regular soldiers as well as a body of Argyll
militiamen. After Culloden, and on resignation of his commission
as an officer, he accepted a Government factorship dealing with con-
fiscated Jacobite estates in Lochaber and in Appin, two regions he
knew well. He also knew intimately lairds and commoners alike
living in these parishes. Initially he was not harsh in his dealings
with the returned and disassembling Jacobites, which was a mark
in his favour, for he was, in fact, under a constant small cloud of
suspicion as to his loyalty to his Government employers. Indeed,
had it been known in official circles that he had given a personal
loan of £500 to such an out-and-out Jacobite as Laurence Oliphant
of Gask, he would have been dismissed summarily. However, the
simple fact that a Campbell with Hanoverian leanings had been
appointed superior over Stewart territory made for some tough
and often awkward problems.

The other personality in the famous case was James Stewart, who
at the time of the crime managed the estates of his half brother,
Charles Stewart, 5th of Ardsheil, who had, after the rising, been
attainted and had escaped to France. James Stewart, known as
Seumas a' Ghlinne (James of the Glen), had been an officer in the
Stewart Brigade during the rising, but as the part he had played
was a minor one, he was pardoned under the Act of Indemnity. He
was a man of considerable ability and natural gifts. The relations between Glenure and Stewart were distinguished by a commendable
spirit of compromise, with Stewart acting as a kind of sub-factor
under Glenure's supervision. However, the degree of cordial-

ity which existed between the two men led to Glenure being suspected of being a secret Jacobite. At a time when 'Pickle the Spy' was active, and fears of another rising and foreign invasion was abroad, a Government agent with such sympathies was the last thing the authorities wanted in Lochaber and in Appin, long known as being hotbeds of Jacobitism.

Glenure was well aware of the situation he was in and in order to right the keel, he decided to display some vigour in his dealings with the late rebels. In 1751 James Stewart was asked to give up the farm of Glenduror where he was settled, receiving in its place the farm of Acharn. His own farm was then settled by a Campbell. James Stewart removed himself with little or no demonstration, though the act rankled him. Often, when he was in his cups, to which he was evidently becoming increasingly addicted, he was in the habit of uttering threats against Glenure, as men still do in these circumstances when the head is misted by whisky fumes. Apparently, he still continued to apply the surplus rents from the tenants on the new farm to the advantage of the exiled Ardsheil family.

Colin Campbell's next move was to warn a number of Jacobite tenants on the Ardsheil estates to move out by Whitsunday 1752. After Glenure had obtained authority from the Sheriff to evict them, James Stewart immediately took up their cause. He had mixed motives for his action: genuine goodness of heart, his undisputed loyalty to the exiled Ardsheil, and the disturbing thought that Stewart lands would be eventually settled by incoming Hanoverian tenants. He went to Edinburgh to petition against the evictions. His memorial was to have been presented to the Exchequer Court in that city, but he found he had missed one sitting, with the next sitting to be held in June—by then it would be too late to oppose by legal means the evictions. Stewart then presented a Bill of Suspension to counter Glenure's Precept of Removal against the Ardsheil tenants. But the Suspension Order was refused.

On Monday 11th May Glenure left home for Fort William to carry out evictions on the estate of Cameron of Locheil, at Mamore, and on Thursday 14th May he set out for Appin, where he was due to carry out evictions on the following day. The position of the tenants in Appin was desperate. There were rumours that Glenure intended to become Laird of Appin and his policies would spell ruin for both gentry and commoner alike.

In the late evening of 14th May, Glenure and his company crossed the ferry at Ballachulish, during which he was persuaded by the ferryman not to take the proposed route through the woods of Lettermore. But Glenure felt he would be safe once he had left Stewart country. Going through the woods, Glenure's companions were strung out as they rode along the road through the wood, still traceable in parts as a grassy track. Suddenly the sound of a shot rang out from behind a bush and Glenure was struck by two bullets entering his back, one on either side of his spine. Mungo Campbell, Glenure's nephew, riding in front, immediately dismounted and eased his uncle off his horse, the latter being in obvious pain and swooning. Mungo Campbell then ran up the hill to see who had fired the shot and saw ". . . at some distance from him, a man with a short dark-coloured coat, and a gun in his hand, going away from him". The shot was fired at about 5.30 p.m. and Glenure died about half an hour later.

There was an immediate sensation caused throughout Appin and the district and a search for the killer started, for there was a growing belief that many were involved in the assassination plot. A number of likely suspects were being mooted as being eligible. One was Allan Breck Stewart who had been a soldier in the French army and had joined the Hanoverian forces, only to desert them for the Jacobite side. In the event, the search involved the close questioning of more than 700 persons, chiefly at the behest of the relatives of Glenure who demanded vengeance on someone. To many Highlanders, both Jacobite and Hanoverian, the likely suspect was Allan Breck, if only on the grounds of his military training and experience in the use of a musket. He, however, had disappeared after the shooting and could not be found. Later he constantly asserted his innocence with convincing vehemence.

As time went by the crime assumed new facets. Someone must have assisted the murderer. If the latter were Allan Breck, then suspicion must surely fall on James Stewart of the Glen, a natural son of old Stewart of Appin, and a known friend and protector of

Allan Breck. James was in any case bound to be implicated in the crime if only on the basis of his being a known Jacobite who collected the tenantry's rents and had them forwarded through intermediaries to the absent chief in his French exile. James must, it was thought, surely know more than he was prepared to admit and was as likely to be, in fact, as guilty as the assassin who fired the fatal shot.

Accordingly, James Stewart and his son, Allen, were arrested. The father was charged formally, not with the actual murder in person, but with being an accessory before the fact. Allan was arrested, as the oldest son of his father and one who was old enough to be in his father's confidence. The pair were taken to Fort William where they lay from 16th May to the beginning of September.

All possible obstacles were interposed to prevent James of the Glen from preparing his defence. By the ordinary procedure, the prisoner could have had his trial speeded up to have it heard in the High Court in Edinburgh where he would have been assured of an impartial hearing and jury. In addition, Stewart was very low in funds, mainly through legal and other expenses he had incurred in Edinburgh acting on behalf of his tenants; he was also faced with further charges in connection with his protest against Glenure's evictions.

The musket shots which killed Glenure then fell into a pond creating ripples which widened to amplify what was more than likely an act of private revenge into a great political crime, an insult to the Government, and a challenge to the Hanoverian dynasty. Within weeks the King, the Ministers, the Law Officers in London and in Edinburgh, were clanned together in their resolve to exact exemplary retribution for the outrage. Embers of hatred smouldering on after the Forty-five were fanned into a new and fantastic flame which demanded the extirpation of the Appin Stewarts as a clan. The MacIans of Glencoe were being remembered.

The trial of James Stewart was held in Inveraray, before a bench of three judges and a jury composed of fifteen jurors, of whom eleven bore the surname Campbell, with four non-Campbell 'jackal' supporters. The Duke of Argyll took a prominent personal part in the proceedings, and at time took the lead, thus usurping the position of the judges, who scarcely took any positive part in the trial; the Duke, however, was in attendance in his position as Lord Justice General of Scotland. The trial lasted from 21st September (Old Style) to 25th September. The verdict was a foregone conclusion. The evidence against Stewart was tainted and submitted in such a way that the Lord Advocate had to bear responsibility for the travesty of justice which occurred in the Court House at Inveraray. The Campbells had decided to make a sacrifice and the more influential the victim the better. Thus, James' son, Allan, was dismissed, though the circumstantial evidence held against him was as strong as that held against his father. James of the Glen was found guilty and condemned to be hanged for a crime which he did not commit, nor instigate, and, so far as real evidence went, did not know was likely to be committed.

After hearing a tirade made against him by the Duke of Argyll, and the sentence pronounced on him, James Stewart said: "I tamely submit to my hard sentence. I forgive the jury, and the witnesses, who have sworn several things falsely against me: and I declare before the great God, and this auditory, that I had no previous knowledge of the murder of Colin Campbell of Glenure, and am as innocent of it as a child unborn. I am not afraid to die; but what grieves me is my character, that after ages should think me capable of such a horrid and barbarous murder." On 5th October, he was removed to Fort William, to await hanging at Ballachulish.

On 7th November 1752 James Stewart was conveyed over the ferry of Ballachulish, only a few miles from his home, and carried to a gibbet erected on a conspicuous eminence on the south side. On the following day he was to be hanged "betwixt the hours of twelve at noon and two afternoon, to be hanged by the neck upon the said gibbet by the hands of an executioner until he be dead; and thereafter to be hung in chains upon the said gibbet".

The eighth day of November turned out to be a dreadful day, with wild tempest and rain, as though Nature herself were crying in despair of the verdict. The weather in fact so delayed the execution party that it was well past noon before the hill was reached, called Cnap a' Chaolais. In a tent erected for the purpose two ministers in attendance prayed with the condemned man and prepared him for his end. When these devotions and intercessions were over, James Stewart proceeded to read aloud his Dying Speech. He recounted the injustices to which he claimed he had been subjected, but in a moderate and restrained form of words. In the most solemn manner he denied that he had been, directly or indirectly, accessory to Glenure's murder, ". . . nor do I know who was the actor". He prayed to God to pardon the jury and the false witnesses ". . . that they may not be charged with my innocent blood . . . I do declare that none of my friends, to my knowledge, ever did plot or concert that murder; and I am persuaded that they never employed any person to accomplish that cowardly action; and I firmly believe, that there is none of my friends who might have a quarrel with that gentleman, but had the honour and resolution to offer him a fairer chance for his life, than to shoot him privately from a bush."

Then he knelt on the ground and read aloud a long written prayer, believed to be Psalm 35, ever since known in these parts as Salm Sheumas a' Ghlinne, the Psalm of James of the Glen. It was an apt choice: "For without cause they have hid me for their net in a pit, which without cause they have digged for my soul . . . False witnesses did rise up: they laid to my charge things that I knew not."

The fierce gale hindered the executioner and his acolytes after the hanging, for the high wind created difficulties for them in hanging the dead man's body in chains, a task which was not fully accomplished until five o'clock in the afternoon. A guard of fifteen soldiers was stationed in a hut near the hill where the gibbet stood, to prevent the body being cut down. A further precaution, the gibbet was strengthened with iron. It was not until April 1754 that the military guard was removed. During a gale on 30th January 1755 the body fell from the gibbet. The parts were wired together, and it was hung up again. In the end, however, successive gales blew the body down, literally bone by bone.

Thereafter tradition takes over. In one story, running in the family of a descendant of James Stewart (Elizabeth Stewart was a daughter of James Stewart and married a MacCallum; their descendants are said to keep the secret of the real murderer's name within the family), the bones were collected one night in 1756 by some Livingstones (one of whom was Neil, grandfather of David Livingstone) of the island of Ulva, off Mull, and buried secretly in Old Duror Church. In a letter to the *Scots Magazine*, in 1976, Mrs Catherine Pape, says: "If you go there you will find, when you have struggled through the shameful tangle of nettles and brambles, a small brass tablet on the inside of the ruined wall of the church. This tablet was erected by my uncle, Donald MacCallum, and a Captain Stewart, after permission had been obtained from Parliament to put a plate above the grave of proscribed man. The identity of the murderer was passed down to each eldest son of the clan in the direct line."

Another local tradition partly contradicts Mrs Pape's family story that the bones were conveyed immediately to Old Duror Church. This tradition has it that in 1756 the three Livingstone brothers decided that the bones of James Stewart required a decent burial. Their plan was for two of them to wait at dead of night by the side of a steep rock standing out from the shore at Lettermore, below the present hotel there. They were to have a boat ready, and if successful in getting possession of the body, they were to convey it to the island of St Munde and bury it there among the MacDonalds. The third brother was to engage the sentry (the military guard over the gibbet by this time having being reduced to one) in conversation, lead him to within earshot of the other two and propose a refreshment in the nearby inn.

The plan succeeded without a hitch. The two brothers hauled down the gibbet, laid it as it was in the boat and cast off. But the tide was flowing at the time and the current carried them to Eilean nah-Iuraich instead of to St Munde's Isle. This rocky isle had a grassy hollow in its centre and there the remains of James Stewart were interred. Whether they are still there or were later removed to Old Duror Church is a matter for further investigation. The gibbet was thrown overboard and a tradition in Ardgour has it that it came ashore on a spit of land below Nos 11 and 12 Clovullin, which was in consequence renamed by the locals Rudha na Croich. Tradition goes on to say that the tenant of No 11 or No 12 used some of the wood for making a cow stall.

Loch Rangag, the
domain of Greysteel

The monument to
James of the Glen
at Ballachulish

The statue of Rob Roy
in Stirling

Balquhidder

Haunted castles: (*above*) Skibo Castle and (*below*) Inveraray Castle with
Loch Fyne in the foreground

Loch Assynt

The River Inver flowing out from Loch Assynt

(*Above*) Wardlaw Church, Kirkhill and (*below*) Loch Arkaig

(*Above*) H.M.S. *Natal* and (*below*) Berriedale, Caithness

(*Above*) Castle Girnigoe, Noss Head, Caithness and (*below*) the River Spey
at Rothiemurchus

After the burial of the bones, the Livingstone brothers turned and rowed across to Morvern, for the discovery of the missing body would result in severe recriminations in Appin. However, Morvern being only a few miles across Loch Linnhe, they decided it would be safer to move farther away and took a croft on the island of Ulva.

Many traditions have grown up around the Appin Murder and even today the affair arouses considerable interest and speculation. Many eminent legal minds have agreed that the trial was a travesty of justice and that the wrong man was punished. The massive amount of detailed obstruction and attention to revenge to which the Campbells were party during the trial, and after the dead man was hanged, point to an uneasy conscience in that clan. The very fact that a military guard was mounted at Ballachulish for many months, while the body rotted away, indicated the obsessive mind of clan vengeance.

In due time a memorial was erected in 1911 by the Stewart Society to the memory of James of the Glen. It stands a block of rough-faced stone atop pointed stone blocks; surmounting these is a rugged stone brought from Stewart's farm, Acharn, said to have served him as a seat while he watched his men working in the fields. The inscription on the monument proclaims the verdict after ages in a few blunt words: "Executed on this spot for a crime of which he was not guilty".

As for the murdered man, a cairn of stones marks the spot on the hillside at Letter Wood where Campbell of Glenure was shot. But there is nothing to indicate the grave in the Ardchattan Priory private cemetery where Glenure was buried, save a margin of red stones.

The Appin Murder case threw two characters into the limelight, each with some kind of claim to fame. One, Allan Breck Stewart, was regarded as one of the most likely suspects for the murder of Colin Campbell and was transfixed for perpetuity in the fiction of R. L. Stevenson, in *Kidnapped* and its sequel *Catriona*. The other man was James Drummond, alias Macgregor, alias James More. He was the third son of the famous Rob Roy Macgregor, and had served both the Hanoverian and Jacobite parties, betraying them both.

H

Allan Breck Stewart has been somewhat romanticized by Stevenson for he had in fact a rather dubious character. He was an early,
and popular, suspect in the general opinion of the countryside
around Appin when news of Colin Campbell's murder was bruited
abroad. He was described as an "idle vagabond". He always passed
the bounds of tolerance when drinking, and, in drunken outbursts,
often uttered wild threats against Glenure (whom he mistakenly
blamed for having informed against him to the military authorities). Then there was the matter of his flight after the murder. He
was in any case a deserter, an unpardoned rebel and a soldier in the
French army actively recruiting for King Louis. However, while the
general consensus of opinion was that he was capable of the murder, that same opinion gave him the credit of making a tidier job
of it; everything needed for immediate flight would have been ready
to hand, and long before the morning following the killing, he
would have been far away across the moor of Rannoch.

Even those who were preparing the case against James Stewart,
a month after the murder, doubted if he were the guilty party. Indeed, Glenure's brother suggested to the Lord Justice Clerk that a
proclamation should be made offering Allan Breck a free pardon
as a deserter on condition that he gave himself up and disclosed
what information he had. However, his movements at the time
of the murder came under scrutiny and were purported to have
been made with the express purpose of discovering Glenure's time-
table. But as that was public knowledge, Allan Breck's travels in
the Ballachulish area and in Glencoe were pointless and deprived
of ulterior motive. The real reason for his movements may have
been the collection of general news and snippets of information
to take back with him when he returned to France.

In the event, the authorities hunted for him with thoroughness
and vigour. Warrants for his arrest were issued all over Perthshire.
Individual houses were raided and pickets posted at strategic points.
A detachment of two hundred men was based on Appin House. The
Forest of Glen Etive, the braes of Glencoe and Rannoch Moor were
all searched, as were the mountain passes through which it was
expected he might escape. H.M. Sloop *Porcupine* was stationed
off the east coast with orders to stop and search outward-bound

shipping. But Allan Breck, whether innocent or guilty, was too cunning for his pursuers and he managed to slip through the net and escaped to safety and France.

Allan had been a soldier in the French army and had joined the Hanoverian forces, but had later deserted these for the Jacobite side. He was the son of Donald Stewart of Inverchomrie in Rannoch and was brought up by James Stewart of the Glen. He joined the British Army and at the Battle of Prestonpans he was taken prisoner, and thereafter served throughout the campaign in the Jacobite Army. On escaping to France he enlisted in Ogilvy's Scottish Regiment. He made frequent return visits to Scotland and acted as intermediary between the exiled Stewart of Ardsheil and his half-brother, conveying rents from the forfeited estates to the attainted proprietor.

While his escape to France could have been construed as an admission of some degree of guilt, he was in any case a deserter and to face a murder charge to boot was too much to contend with, apart from stretching the arm of destiny just a little too far if he was to keep his head.

In the Appin Murder affair one witness for the prosecution's case against James Stewart of the Glen who in fact did not appear at the Court House in Inveraray in 1752 was James Drummond, alias Macgregor. The third son of Rob Roy Macgregor, he, like Allan Breck, had served in both the Hanoverian and Jacobite forces. He had shared in the abduction of Jean Key, a young widow and heiress, and in her enforced marriage to his brother Robin Oig Macgregor. He was arrested and charged with what was then a capital offence. But the chief witness against him, the young woman herself, died of smallpox on 4th October 1751, before the trial took place, though her judicial declarations were before the Court. James More Macgregor was found guilty, but his jury petitioned against a capital sentence on the grounds that the woman "did afterwards acquiesce". Accordingly, the sentence due to be pronounced was postponed for a period.

While awaiting sentence, James More got into communication with Glenure's brother and offered to swear, in return for a pardon, that James Stewart had tried to persuade him to arrange for the

murder of Glenure at the hands of his brother Robin Oig, an outlaw still at liberty. James Stewart, so the story would be told,
promised to provide the murderer with a good gun and money for
his escape to France where, by Ardsheil's influence, he would be
rewarded with either a commission in the French service, or a pen-
sion, whichever of them he chose.

Glenure's brother, to his discredit, grasped at the chance to
consolidate the slender evidence against James Stewart and a
memorial, setting out the details of the alleged plot, was presented
in Edinburgh, together with a petition for a pardon for James
More. But things did not go so smoothly for either the Campbells
or James More. The authorities in Edinburgh were doubtful
whether he could be pardoned for his crime, and there was the
further real possibility that James More's story could be exposed
for what it was by a thorough cross examination. In the event,
on 16th November James More Macgregor escaped from Edinburgh Castle—where he had been transferred from the city's Tolbooth—by changing clothes with his daughter Elizabeth (Stevenson's Catriona) who had visited him in the disguise of a cobbler.
It was alleged at the time that the escape was connived at by the
Government. If so, the underlings who allowed the escape were
unjustly punished for, by sentence of a court martial, the two
lieutenants of the guard were "broke"; the sergeant "reduced to
a private man"; and the porter was "whipped".

The Balquhidder district of the Trossachs was once the country
of the MacLarens (the surname is spelt MacLaurins on the older
tombstones in the kirkyard). The clan claimed to have received
the lands from one of the early Scottish Kings, Kenneth III. In the
Middle Ages, however, the Macgregors, who came in from the north
and west, succeeded in establishing themselves around Loch Voil,
and the MacLarens, though never completely deposed, began to
wane by about the end of the fifteenth century. The beginning of
the end came when they incurred the enmity of the royal Stewarts,
resulting in James IV confiscating much of their territory. The
Macgregors on the other hand waxed somewhat and the first half
of the sixteenth century saw a Macgregor chief entitled Lord of
Balquhidder.

Inevitably there was a constant warring between the MacLarens and the Macgregors, starting from a bloody clan fight which took place near the Kirkton in the thirteenth century. The trouble arose at one of the famous Balquhidder fairs. A strong band of Mac-Larens, seeking revenge for an insult to one of their clan, attacked a party of Buchanans from Leny, and a fierce struggle ensued, during which the hand was struck off one of the Buchanans. His son picked it up and ran with it down Strathyre to Kilmahog, to show it to his grandfather. In no time at all, the Buchanans rushed down reinforcements to the spot where the MacLarens were worn down by sheer weight of numbers. At this point a band of Mac-gregors, who had till then taken no part in the fight, offered to intervene if the MacLarens would allow them to share the privilege of entering Balquhidder Kirk before the rest of the congregation. The terms were accepted and the Buchanans were soon over-whelmed and pressed back to a loop of the River Balvaig. One by one they were driven over a waterfall into a deep pool, where they were either drowned or killed as they struggled to get out of the water.

The Macgregors, while their star was in the ascendant, were never far from trouble; for centuries the clan was persecuted by the Campbells. As early as the reign of David II, the Campbells managed to procure a legal title to some Macgregor territory. When the Macgregors, after the manner of simple but determined moun-tain folk, defended their land with claymore and dirk, without re-gard to the finer points of the law, their wily opponents obtained writs of the Crown against them so that, as Skene in his *History of the Highlands* says: ". . . the history of the Macgregors consists of a mere list of acts of Privy Council by which commissions are granted to pursue the clan with fire and sword, and of various atrocities which a state of desperation, the natural result of these measures, as well as a deep spirit of vengeance against both the framers and the executioners of them, frequently led the clan to commit".

Finally the Macgregors were proscribed, obliged under pain of death to change their surname, forbidden to carry any weapons save a knife without a point to cut their food, or to meet together in greater number than four at a time—and the execution of these commands was entrusted to the clan's hereditary foes, the Campbells. These laws remained in force until the end of the eighteenth century, when they were all repealed by the Parliament of 1784. In spite of all the efforts of their enemies, strong bands of Macgregors held out in the high mountains and rocky fastnesses, and were able to muster considerable forces as their contribution to the risings of 1715 and 1745. Many are the tales of generosity and courage told on the part of these persecuted people, and through these they are shown off to far greater advantage than their treacherous and cunning enemies.

One well-known tale which brings the Macgregors into an honourable light is worth recording. The son of Macgregor of Glen Strae was out hunting one day and by chance fell in with the young Laird of Lamont and a companion travelling towards Inverlochy. They passed the day together and in the evening sat down to dinner. But during the course of the meal a quarrel arose, dirks were drawn and young Macgregor was killed. Lamont at once leapt out of the room and fled, closely pursued by some of the dead man's retainers. Fleet of foot, he outstripped his foes and, by chance, ran for protection to the very house of Glen Strae where young Macgregor's father lived. Without stating whom he had slain, Lamont implored Glen Strae's assistance. At once the old chief passed the word that he was to be protected. Almost directly the members of the clan arrived in hot pursuit and angrily cried out for the murderer to be handed over to them, to make him pay for the blood he had shed. But the old chief, on hearing whom he was sheltering in his house, said, "Not a hair of his head shall be touched while he is under my roof-tree. Glen Strae has pledged his honour, and never shall it be said that a Macgregor went back on his word." Later the chief secretly escorted Lamont out of Macgregor country to his own lands and, bidding him farewell, said: "Lamont, you are now safe upon your own ground. I cannot and will not protect you further. Keep away from my people, and may God forgive you what you have done." Lamont was not ungrateful, and shortly afterwards, when Glen Strae and his family were proscribed, destitute, and reduced to the status of wanderers, Lamont received

them into his own house, an offence in itself, and for a time protected them. But in the event, the honest old chief was treacher-
ously done to death by the Earl of Argyll and hanged at the Market
Cross in Edinburgh.

Balquhidder is well known and visited each year by tourists
attracted to the grave of Rob Roy Macgregor, which is in fact a
family grave, for with him lie buried his wife and two of his five
sons, Coll and Robert (Robin Oig). Sir Walter Scott, in his long introduction to his *Rob Roy*, stated that Macgregor's dates of birth
and death were uncertain. But in fact they are known to within a
few days. Towards the turn of this century a record of Rob Roy's
baptism was found in the registers of the Parish of Buchanan. The
entry states that he was baptized Robert, son of Donald Macgregor
and Margaret Campbell, on 7th March 1671. Donald Macgregor
presented himself "upon testificat" from the Minister of Callander, in whose parish he resided. Why Rob Roy's father had to go
to the minister of the adjoining Parish of Buchanan is not clear,
unless it was due to his own parish minister refusing to baptize
the child with the proscribed name of Macgregor and thereby
exposing himself to legal penalties—though this is unlikely for
the punitive Act was at that time in abeyance. Donald Macgregor
had lands in Glengyle and was a soldier of some distinction; in
the army of James II he rose to the rank of Lieutenant-Colonel.
Margaret Campbell, Rob Roy's mother, was a daughter of a neighbouring laird, Campbell of Glenfalloch. More than likely Rob Roy
was born in Glengyle. He died in Balquhidder, at the farmhouse of
Inverlochlarig Beag, round about the 28th December 1734. This
date is fixed by a notice which appeared in a special edition of the
Caledonian Mercury of 9th January 1735: "On Saturday was
se'night [i.e., a week ago last Saturday] died at Balquhidder in
Perthshire the famed Highland partizan Rob Roy."

Of all Highland warriors perhaps Rob Roy Macgregor is the
most famous, immortalized in books of fact and fiction; as a
champion of his clan and clan name, the Macgregors had no better.
His early life was uneventful; he received an education which, while
not particularly liberal, was regarded as being sufficient for him to
fulfil the quiet avocations of the rural life it was intended he

should lead. However, he did excel in some subjects, including the broadsword and the ancient history and language of his country. He helped his father in tending to the estates and collecting rents and black-mail, payments for the protection he offered to surrounding proprietors. In raising the black-mail tax, Rob Roy was sanctioned, if not by Act of Parliament, at least by custom and local institution. He was for some time employed in assisting the police of the different surrounding districts in collecting imposts that were paid for the maintenance of the 'Black Watch', a corps of provincial militia whose duty it was to protect the lives and properties of the local people from distant plunderers. The corps, wholly composed of Highlanders, was supported by levies. The independent companies of the Black Watch afterwards became companies of regular troops, and were the origin of the gallant 42nd Regiment of Foot, for a long time known by the name of the Highland Watch. His strength, courage, and no-nonsense manner in dealing with problems soon won for him a wide reputation, so much so that when the great families of Montrose and Argyll, long at variance on political topics, fell out on personal grounds, both were eager to gain the friendship of Rob Roy. His independent mind, daring spirit and the general esteem in which he was held, could make him an ideal friend or a dangerous enemy.

Montrose was his near neighbour and he set about cultivating Rob Roy by suggesting that they become partners in the trade of cattle dealing, to which Rob Roy agreed. Argyll, on the other hand, had a problem to solve first: his own clan's centuries of cruelties and injustices perpetrated against the Clan Gregor. One glimmer of hope for Argyll lay in the fact that, due to the surname of Macgregor being proscribed, Rob Roy had taken the surname Campbell, though this was in respect of his mother and in compliance with the law and not because Rob Roy was particularly enamoured of carrying an obnoxious name. Argyll found his overtures to Rob Roy spurned: old feuds and history still burned painfully bright in the hearts and minds of the Macgregors. But then an incident occurred which caused a rift between Montrose and Rob Roy, and the latter veered towards Argyll. The incident involved a Macdonald, an inferior partner in the cattle-dealing venture, who, entrusted with a large sum of money, fled the country with the lot and eluded pursuit. The responsibility for the money was Rob Roy's; but Montrose refused to accept that he was not entirely to blame, and laid the loss at Rob Roy's door, who was forced to make over his property to Montrose to satisfy the claim, on the understanding that should circumstances and finances permit, Rob Roy would obtain control over his lands again. But when the situation did eventually arise, Montrose put both financial and legal obstacles in the way, with the result that Rob Roy was ultimately deprived of his property. Argyll now became a friend of Rob Roy and cultivated the latter. But this association was being watched by Montrose who wrote Rob Roy to the effect that he might gain substantially if he were to go to Edinburgh and inform of the political dealings in which Argyll was engaged. Rob Roy refused and for this he was finally evicted from his estate.

Rob Roy was now in a furious rage. His family had been evicted in his absence, in shameful circumstances. His wife, in particular, was treated savagely, an outrage which Rob Roy never forgave and which became the basis for the measures of retaliation he afterwards adopted. He 'collected' the rents which were due to Montrose at Term times and kept these for himself. At first Montrose overlooked these acts, realizing that in his treatment of Rob Roy he had been more than unjust. However one final act of 'collection' brought matters to a head. Montrose's factor was one day collecting rents at Chapellaroch in Stirlingshire when he was confronted by Rob Roy at the head of a band of eager men. He was forced to hand over a huge sum of money, for which Rob Roy gave a receipt. The sum involved was too large to be ignored and Montrose became a firm and resolute enemy of Rob Roy Macgregor.

From then on Rob Roy was ever in trouble, much of it with a political flavour; even so he had a high regard for justice and honour and was rarely in a position to be accused of treachery.

In March 1719 a Proclamation was issued against him. The date is significant. Ormonde's expedition, which terminated fatally at Glensheil in the following June, had already set sail from France, and the Hanoverians were well aware that a rising in the North of Scotland was imminent. Almost instinctively their suspicions fell on Rob Roy as the man most likely to be concerned in it, since his activities had fanned the flame of rebellion long after the Jacobite cause had assumed a hopeless aspect. It was most likely the intention of the Government was to direct special measures against him before Ormonde or Marischall could land in Scotland, so as to prevent Rob Roy from joining either of them. The crime with which Rob Roy was charged was a simple criminal offence and did not warrant regal interference; it could quite easily have been dealt with by the Lord Advocate for Scotland. Yet the Proclamation was dated from "Our Court at St James", as though a murder in Scotland could not be published by ordinary legal procedures.

When the Proclamation was published "at the Mercat Cross of Inveraray" Rob Roy was in the immediate neighbourhood mustering the Breadalbane Campbells, the Macgregors and the Murrays, to join the Spanish Auxiliaries under Earl Marischall. The Proclamation did little other than to confirm Rob Roy's opposition to Hanoverian rule in Scotland. It is no slight testimony to the steadfastness of his adherents that the magnificent offers of reward were powerless to seduce them from their fidelity (a common Highland trait). "Two hundred pounds sterling"—the price put on Rob Roy's head—would have been a real fortune in those days for any traitor; but none was found. The Proclamation begins: "Dieu et mon Droit – BY THE KING. A PROCLAMATION for the discovering and apprehending Robert Campbell, alias Macgregor, commonly called Rob Roy, for the several crimes therein mentioned. George R."

The document then details of a raid on a house by Rob Roy and his band in which there was an officer and twenty men, with others, all followers of the Duke of Montrose. One man was killed. It was a kind of activity that was fairly common; yet it drew the attention of the King.

His life was full with never a dull moment and the wonder is that he managed to live until his sixties. He was never one to refuse a challenge to a duel, depending on the strength of his arms to see him through an encounter when his opponent was the better swordsman. He was in fact very strong and was known to seize a deer by the horns and hold it fast. His arms were long, almost to the point of deformity, "when he stood erect he could touch the garters under his knee with his fingers". One of his duelling opponents was Stewart of Ardsheil, who beat him fairly and caused Rob Roy to vow that he would never take up the sword again, though this incident occurred when he was old.

He was a larger-than-life character while he lived; after his death he grew in stature as being one of the last of the genuine Highlanders of the old stock, who longed to support the ancient privileges and independence of the Gaelic race. He hated double-dealing. Although when in warfare he may not have always adhered to the niceties of justice, yet he was often known to exercise mercy, even at the risk of his own life. Of his being a freebooter, and heading a band of desperate *banditti*, there is no proof. He was never known to have provoked an unwarranted attack, or to have broken any promise he gave. He was generous to a fault. It was these qualities which brought him to the notice of many after his death, the subject of novels and the like.

When Dorothy Wordsworth returned to the Trossachs in 1822 a peculiar amalgam of the histrionic and the mercenary held sway. Thanks to the literary efforts of Sir Walter Scott, Highland Scotland had become 'Scotland' and Rob Roy's cave a place of mindless pilgrimage:

> Our Highland Musician tunes his pipes as we approach Rob Roy's Caves. The grandeur of nature strangely mixed up with Stage effects; but it is good acting—not of the Surrey Theatre. An old Highlander, with long grey locks, bonnet, and plaid, is seated on one of the crags. Boys at different heights with bags of fresh-gathered nuts. Every passenger leaves the Boat, and what a scramble among rocks and trees! A Piper in his Tartan Robes is still playing a rouzing tune. All press forward to Rob Roy's Cave, as it is called, pass through in succession, the Cave being so small that not more than two or three can enter at once, and having an outlet at the other side. We flatter ourselves we make a wiser choice in not entering at all; for they profess to have no motive but to *say* that have been in Rob Roy's cave because Sir Walter Scott has made

them so much talked about; and, when they come out, dashing
the dust off their cloaths, the best they can say is "Well! there is
nothing to be seen; but it is worthwhile, if only to *say* that one
has been there!"

The great-great-great-great-great-grandson of Rob Roy Macgregor, Mr Adam Macgregor Dick, of Kilmarnock, had one ambition: a statue of his illustrious descendant to be raised in
perpetual memory of the famous Highlander. Unhappily he did not
live to see the final work unveiled. It stands in Stirling, not Balquhidder, as might have been expected. It was executed by the
sculptor Mr Benno Schotz, who went to great pains over the research needed to produce an authenticated statue; the length of
the arms in particular was a feature of the research. A plaque on
the base simply states: "Rob Roy; Born at Glengyle and Baptized
7th March 1671; Died at Balquhidder, 28th December 1734; 'My
Foot is on my Native Heath, And My Name it is MacGregor' ".

Rob Roy had several children, including some sons who, in their
own way, laid some claim to fame. One of these was Robin Oig,
the youngest and favourite of Rob Roy. On a cold February day in
1754, he stood on the scaffold in Edinburgh's Grassmarket. He had
just finished his confession and nodded to the executioner who
stepped forward to carry out his duty, and the condemned man
departed this life with dignity—much to the disappointment of the
large crowd gathered to watch, half expecting the son of Rob Roy
Macgregor to make a histrionic display for their benefit. The body
was cut down by friends, dressed in the garb of a Highland chief;
then a small procession escorted the body on the long road back
to Balquhidder where Robin Oig was interred in the family grave.

The road taken by Robin Oig Macgregor to the Edinburgh
scaffold was a tortuous one, begun at the age of seventeen, twenty
years previously. At a young age he had fallen under the influence
of his notorious elder brother, James More and soon was running
wild with a pack of caterans who pillaged the countryside. His
other brothers were also participants in these forays, but eventually they accepted their father's recommendation to take the King's
Peace and settle down in Balquhidder.

On the death of Rob Roy, James More assumed the headship of

the family and continued to exert bad influences on all around him. In particular he persuaded Robin Oig to kill a John MacLaren, who had obtained the tenancy of a farm which the Macgregors regarded as theirs. Reluctantly the young Robin took an old Spanish flintlock belonging to his father and shot MacLaren as the latter was plough- ing the disputed fields. James More had, however, forgotten that with the passage of the years, the arm of the law in Scotland was well able to reach into the lands of Balquhidder and before he realized it, he and his brothers were summoned to the High Court in Edinburgh to stand trial for murder. The brothers were found by the jury to keep the peace for seven years on sureties of £200 each, after a verdict of 'not proven' was given.

Robin then found himself in France becoming involved with exiled Jacobites in Paris; but life was difficult through a shortage of funds. Eventually he enlisted in the Hanoverian army, to fight at the bloody Battle of Fontenoy in 1744, where he was captured by the French. Exchanged in 1745, he returned to Scotland and joined the Black Watch, unwittingly fighting against James More at Culloden. After the rising, he was discharged and returned to Balquhidder. He married the daughter of the Laird of Drunkie (the man whose cattle was allegedly stolen by Rob Roy and which deed, with the killing of a man, was the subject of a King's Proclamation against Rob Roy). But the farm on which the couple were settled failed and, turning his hand to other ventures, found failure at every turn. His young wife died in 1750, leaving him in despair and burdened with debt. His brother, James More, then entered on stage, with the suggestion that the solution to all prob- lems was the marrying of an heiress. There was one such at Eden- bellie, called Jean Key. The elder brother insisted that Robin Oig visit her and propose marriage. Robin was more than reluctant to do this but was persuaded by his brother's forceful arguments. So he set off for Edenbellie farm, where Jean Key lived, with estates worth 20,000 Scots merks and an income of 2,000 merks annually. She had been widowed only recently, after a marriage lasting some ten months.

Robin duly presented himself and his suit, but was brushed off by the young lady and her aunt and uncle. The Macgregors were regarded as little more than thieves. Rebuffed Robin Oig made his way back to Balquhidder to tell the tale. As he expected James More flew into a rage, more from the loss of probable income than from the insult. He gathered a band of his old cronies, forced Robin and his other brother Colin to accompany them, and set off hot-foot for Edenbellie. The Key family were sitting at supper when the door burst open and rough Highlanders poured into the room. Jean Key was extricated from a cupboard, where she had gone into hiding, and taken outside, to be put on a horse. The party made for Drymen, where James More despatched a letter to Glasgow asking a friend to bring a priest to Rowardennan on Lochlomondside by the following Monday morning. The purpose was to marry off Robin Oig and the poor reluctant widow. In due time a priest arrived—though he may have been an impostor arranged by James More—and the wedding ceremony went ahead in the presence of witnesses who were later to testify that Jean Key had responded freely to the priest's questions as to her free will. Then followed a weary tour round the countryside, during which time, warrants were issued against the Macgregors. Then it was home to Balquhidder, where the couple were tested by the Kirk Session to ascertain that they were truly man and wife; three elders were later to testify that both answered freely and in the affirmative. James More then decided that it was best for the matter to be formalized in Edinburgh where the case was to be presented before the courts. But the affair proved a web of complicated action and counter-action with Jean Key saying at one turn that she was Robin's wife and wished to remain so, and at another, that she had been abducted and forced to marry.

After much to-ing and fro-ing, James More was arrested and imprisoned in Edinburgh Castle, while Robin Oig managed to flee in time to escape arrest. Jean returned to Glasgow with her mother but, worn out by her experiences and enforced travels, she contracted smallpox and died five months later in October 1751, aged only twenty years. She was buried in Kippen Churchyard, where her gravestone can still be seen.

James More then found himself standing trial on charges of hamesucken (armed housebreaking) and forcible abduction and the jury issued one of the oddest verdicts in Scottish legal history: he was found guilty of the first charge but not of the second. There was some doubt about Jean Key's involvement in the affair (a letter had been produced, probably forged, which was written in Robin's favour) and the sentence was deferred for five months. During this time James More made a daring escape from Edinburgh Castle and fled to France where he died in abject poverty in 1754.

As for Robin Oig, he was eventually captured at Gartmore and he stood trial on 24th December 1753. The jury again stood on its head to bring forward the verdict that Robin Oig was guilty of hamesucken and forcible abduction but not guilty of rape or forcible marriage. However, the first two charges carried the death sentence and he was duly sentenced to be hung. His last words on the scaffold were to hope that his death would be an expiation for the sins of his elder brother, who had been instrumental in bringing him there. Thus the least guilty of all Rob Roy's sons paid with his life in February 1754.

During the early years of last century the island of Lewis and Harris was plagued by a robber and murderer called Mac-an-t-Sronaich. Though he looms large in Lewis tradition, he is in fact a rather shadowy figure. His origins vary from being a Donald Cameron, on the run from Lochaber, to a Stronach from Loch Broom, in Wester Ross. He flourished in the 1830s, with indications that he was a fugitive from justice; one tradition is that he was responsible for the death of a servant girl in his father's house. So far as the Law was concerned there was a character roaming about the Lewis moors causing trouble:

Procurator Fiscal v. Bodach na Monach or Famtom. A Moor Stalker.
Unto the Honourable the Sheriff of Ross-shire or his Substitute for the Lewis district, the Petition of Thomas Buchanan Drummond, Writer in Stornoway, Proc. Fiscal of Court for the said District.
Humbly sheweth. That the petitioner has received information of there being a man lurking about in the island of Lewis who is suspected of having committed some serious crime but for the present has evaded being brought to justice, and as he puts the inhabitants of the Island in fear of their lives (he being armed with dangerous weapons) besides, as their sheep and cattle may be destroyed and their goods seized and carried off by that person, who

at present can have no lawful means of procuring subsistence, and hence the petitioner suspects him either to be a criminal escaped from justice, Vagabond, or Plunderer, which renders the present application necessary, May it therefore please Your Lordship to consider what is above set forth, and in respect of the peculiar circumstances of the case, grants warrants to Officers of Court, Constables, their Concurrents, and to any of the Natives of the Island to pass search form and apprehend the person referred to, and to bring him before you for examination, and thereafter, upon advising again this application with the declaration of the accused and other evidence that may be adduced, do and determine in the premises as to your Lordship shall seem proper.

The petition is dated 8th July 1834. There is nothing in the legal records to indicate that the warrant was ever executed and it would appear that Mac-an-t-Sronaich gave the Officers of the Court and other executors of the Law the slip. Tradition says that he managed to secrete himself on board a sailing packet bound from Stornoway to Lochewe and disappeared from the island. Yet another tradition suggests that he was eventually caught and formally charged, before being transferred to the mainland where, after trial, he was executed.

Whatever the final fate of the outlaw, his stay on Lewis caught the island by the ears and placed the inhabitants in a state of great fear and alarm. Many and varied are the traditional tales of the man's exploits. He is credited with having killed a man for the sake of the jar of whisky he carried. The locale ranges from just outside Stornoway to Ardhasaig, in North Harris. One day a herd boy was accosted by Mac-an-t-Sronaich who asked if the former had any food. The lad handed over his poor fare which was quickly eaten by the robber. Asking if the lad had any more food, he received a reply in the negative whereupon the outlaw became angry and threw the boy into a nearby loch where he drowned. When finally Mac-na-t-Sronaich was caught, it is said that of all his crimes, the death of the herd boy was the one he most regretted.

The outlaw met his match one day on the road between Stornoway and Barvas, on the west of the island, in the form of a rather well-built lad of seventeen, strong as a horse. He was accosted by the outlaw and a struggle ensued which ended with the lad gaining possession of the outlaw's knife, the 'Sgian Mhort', which for years afterwards was a prized possession until it was lost overboard from one of the local fishing boats.

Perhaps the fact that the final days of Mac-an-t-Sronaich are shrouded in the mist of tradition is appropriate, for all those who lived beyond the law tended to be larger than life, and who followed lifestyles which were unacceptable to the normal Highlander. Yet, there may be bound up in many of these characters an ideal of freedom from the restraints which society, in its development, has always imposed on those who are more law-abiding. Otherwise, one must explain the romance which surrounds many freebooters in Highland history, not all of it deserved, but nevertheless generated by popular acclaim.

FIVE

Accusing Fingers

The ghost is deeply embedded in the folklore and tradition of the Scottish Highlands and Islands. Its role is varied: from merely haunting buildings bemoaning its fate, to warning the living of some impending disaster. But on occasion a troubled spirit has entered into the lives of the living to some purpose, particularly to obtain some satisfaction in the procurement of a final resting place, or to obtain revenge for wrongs done during its own lifetime. Extrapolating from the ghost, the ability to look back to a past time and to peer forward into the future—in itself a kind of time-warping—has made its own contribution not only to Highland lore but to the legal records of trials in Scotland. These instances may seem far-fetched until one realizes that in our own time clairvoyants have been employed by police to locate missing persons, often long dead, the victim of murder, and to produce clues which eventually lead to the conviction of a killer. In the more credulous times of a century ago or so, these things were normal and acceptable; today they are strange and mysterious. Many Highland districts have a well-known local spot where murdered pedlars have stopped a passerby to hold him in thrall until cock-crow, while the tale of some dastardly deed was told in all its gruesome detail.

The truth is often stranger than fiction, and when this occurs in such a staid and unbending context as a Scottish Court of Law, the truth must often be seen to be defiant of any logic. Yet there is recorded in the annals of Scottish legal history the strange case of Sergeant Davies's ghost. The year was 1759 when, despite some three years of military subjugation, the unruly Highlands had not yet been pacified, though the methods used to achieve this aim were often beyond description in the suffering caused to many innocents. The spirit of the clans was abroad and, though the hills might seem lonely at first glance, in fact they were alive with people hiding from the red-coated soldiers, and skulking in caves, hollows and the wooded parts of the glens. One evening in the summer of 1749, Sergeant Davies, of Guise's Regiment, marched from Aberdeen to Dubrach, in Braemar, with a party of eight privates. The business of the mission was to conduct a general surveillance in the district and particularly to obtain information of any disaffected person who might be hiding in the district. The sergeant was a popular man, well-liked and newly-married. His wife, who was later called to bear witness in Edinburgh, swore that "he and she lived together in as great amity and love as any couple could do, and that he was never willing to stay away a night from her".

On the 28th September, Sergeant Davies and his party met up with John Gower in Glenclunie; the latter was wearing a tartan coat. This was, at that time, proscribed dress, and Davies, according to his nature, though this was in defiance of the law, advised him not to use the dress in public. He then dismissed Gower with a warning, rather than take him prisoner. Shortly after this incident, Davies left his men to try for a shot at a stag he had seen. He was never seen again. His men searched for him without success and they returned to report the matter to their commanding officer. Later, with a much enlarged search party, the hills in the area were scoured, but no trace of the missing sergeant was ever discovered.

In the following year, 1750, a shepherd, Alexander Macpherson, made it known that he was being "greatly troubled by the ghost of Sergeant Davies who had insisted that he should bury his bones". Macpherson was at first dismissed as being someone lacking in the head, until he persisted with his story. The ghost then instructed Macpherson to contact a Donald Farquharson, with whom Davies had once lodged. Macpherson did as requested by the troubled spirit and, with Farquharson's help, with some clues offered by the ghost, the sergeant's bones were eventually found buried in peat moss. That was a startling outcome. But more was to follow.

The ghost appeared once again and conveyed information to Macpherson that two men were responsible for his death, one Duncan Clerk and an Alexander Bain MacDonald. The authorities, though reluctant to act on this information, were sufficiently impressed by the manner in which the body was found and decided to arrest the two named men, who were taken to Edinburgh to be lodged in the Tolbooth there in September 1753 on various charges, including the wearing of the kilt.

In the following year they were tried, against evidence produced which suggested that they had indeed killed the sergeant. The two men naturally denied the crime and their insistence, coupled with a defence which pleaded logic rather than a belief in the supernatural, led to their acquittal. Thus, for all its trouble, the ghost of Sergeant Davies failed to get satisfaction from the land of the living. Even so, it was said that the two accused men led miserable lives after their trial and perhaps the ghostly visitor had its due revenge in the end.

A common practice in olden times was that of compelling suspected murderers to touch the dead body of the victim, under the impression that it would bleed afresh at the touch of the guilty person. In the case that follows, it was the only evidence, startling and impressive, on which a man was committed to prison and treated with barbarity and neglect. In 1643, in Wardlaw, Kirkhill, near Inverness, a farm foreman, John MacIan Mhor, was threshing straw for cattle. It was the common practice to make hampers of straw stalks, which he was allowed by his employer to do. But the practice went further one day when, filling a small sack with barley, he put it into the hamper and made off home. But he was seen by a boy, Donald MacWilliam, a labourer on the same farm, who, with a characteristic horror of dishonesty said: "This is not honest; you abuse the trust which your master gives you." MacIan became afraid at this and plotted to keep his deed a secret. He told MacWilliam that he would be well rewarded for his silence—from the proceeds of a seal which he had found by the shore and for which he would be paid a good price. MacWilliam's silence for a share was the offer and after some persuading MacWilliam agreed. Later that night MacWilliam went to the place designated for the meeting with MacIan, who also took along with him his brother-in-law, to help him carry out what he had in mind for MacWilliam. The latter met the two men and before he had a chance to speak fell back with a dirk in his heart which MacIan placed therewith a lunge full of hatred and fear. The brother-in-law, John Mac-Kenzie, was shocked. But he was persuaded by MacIan to "give him the next stab so that you may be as deep in the guilt as I am". MacKenzie did so and completed the death of the lad MacWilliam. The pair of killers then took the body to the shore, hoping that the sea would remove it and carry it far off.

But the sea did not play its intended part. On the third day after the killing, the body was found and carried to Wardlaw Church. The Sheriff, Alexander Chisholm, was sent for and on his arrival, the whole parish was convened. The body was stripped and laid out on a plank, at the entry to the chapel. All of the parishioners were called out, and everyone was summoned to touch the body. Almost 700 names were called before that of John MacIan Mhor was raised. Confidently, he stepped up to the body and laid his hand on the cold bare breast of the victim. No sooner had he done so when the biggest wound opened and a drop of blood was seen to ooze out. Those present were astounded, more so than MacIan; and to make sure, the assembled crowd forced MacIan to repeat the act. Again blood oozed from the wound. MacIan was then seized and carried into the church. After a prayer, he was examined with the threat of torture. But he resisted all attempts to wring a confession out of him. He was then taken to Inverness Prison. As for Mac-Kenzie, that bird had flown, being last seen at the bridge in Inverness, buying ground tobacco, and then making his way through Strathnairn, to the south-east. For two years nothing was heard or seen of him.

Meanwhile, MacIan was put into the stocks in a pit and was there for about a fortnight. The stocks, however, did more than hold him, for his ankles were secured so tightly that they prevented circulation of the blood, and, being thus deprived, the poor man's feet fell off. This happening excited the sympathy of the community (he had not confessed his guilt so there was doubt as to his innocence) and he was released, being taken on a sledge through the streets of Inverness and out into the countryside to his house at Fingask where his wife and friends attended him. Later, when his stumps had healed, he became a beggar and was a common sight in the district.

John MacKenzie was eventually discovered, by an amazing chance and quirk of Fate. A doctor from Inverness happened to be in the company of the minister of the Parish of Keith in Banffshire, with whom he discussed the murder in the course of conversation. He described MacKenzie and was startled to hear the parson say that a man fitting the description was in that very parish. Later that night a man was apprehended and identified as MacKenzie. After being thoroughly interrogated, he confessed to the murder, implicating MacIan, who was re-arrested. Both men were taken to the Castle Hill of Inverness for trial.

MacIan was beheaded at the block at the hands of the common hangman; his body was buried under the gallows and his head was put on one of the spikes at the Tolbooth of Inverness. His right hand was cut off and sent to Wardlaw parish, to be placed on a pike near, and in view of, Wardlaw Church. MacKenzie was sent to Wardlaw parish to be beheaded. His head accompanied MacIan's on the same pole. Thus, did a superstitious belief reveal two cruel murderers.

Rait Castle, about three miles south of Nairn, once belonged to the Cummings or Comyn family. They invited the Mackintoshes to a feast at Rait, intending to murder them. But the latter, who were forewarned, came armed and prepared for treachery. The Chief of the Cummings, whose daughter was in love with a Mackintosh, suspected her of the betrayal and cut off her hands. Terrorized, she leaped to her death from the castle tower. Since then the castle has stood gaunt and empty—save for the ghost of a girl in a bloodstained dress and with no hands, and always accompanied by the eerie clash of steel on stone. Another building which has a powerful atmosphere about it is Saddell Abbey; sensitives have noticed its pervading mood which soaks into the body and mind like a clammy, cold mist, to prove, perhaps, that the abbey has seen, in its former times, sights of tragedy. Its walls have absorbed the sounds of its past and these now slowly exude from the stonework. Spectres have been seen, with lights and the occasional unexplained sound. Inveraray Castle is haunted by the ghost of a harper who was hanged at Inveraray by Montrose; but as the present house was not built until the mid-eighteenth century, presumably he was hanged on the site which was, in fact, once known as Gallows Foreland Point. The harper's ghost has been both seen and heard, and his presence has been felt in Archie's Room, the Blue Room, the Green Library, and on the stairs. Skibo Castle is said to be haunted by a murdered woman whose screams are said to be heard on still dark nights.

One Highland legend tells of the time when the Mackintoshes patched up their long-standing quarrel with the Grants and swore to maintain the peace. However, they captured two Grants and then asked the daughter of one of them, who was betrothed to the other, which should die: her father or her lover. Distraught, she eventually decided to let her father be killed, only to see them both murdered before her eyes. Not unnaturally, she cursed the Mackintoshes of Moy that they should never again have a direct heir. This has not entirely been fulfilled, but Moy has passed rather more frequently to a brother, nephew or a cousin during the past two hundred years. The Curse of Moy was made famous by Sir Walter Scott. He wrote of the celebration at the birth of a Mackintosh heir when the ghost of Margaret Grant appeared and cursed the child: "The blast of death is on the heath...."

The ghost in Duntrune Castle, Argyll, haunts the rooms with a tragedy he has trailed behind him through the years. The story has it that a piper was sent to the castle by Left-handed Col, in the seventeenth century to spy out the land. But he was captured and imprisoned in a turret room. His pipes were thrown in after him. These, however, he used to good effect by playing "The Piper's Warning to his Master" (in another version of the story it was "The Campbells are Coming"). Campbell of Duntrune then had the piper's hands cut off and the poor man died instantly with the shock. But his warning had been heard and Duntrune's plans went agley. For a long time after the Campbells had emigrated to Australia, and the castle had fallen into ruins, the sound of pipes were often heard. The castle was later restored and during the renovations two skeleton hands were discovered under the kitchen floor. Duntulm Castle is haunted by a cousin of the Lord of the Isles who tried to usurp the latter's position. For his efforts, he was walled up in the tower with a piece of salt beef and an empty water jug. His skeleton was found years later. This technique of killing was quite common in the Highlands as a means of persuasion for one purpose or another.

One night many years ago a man named John was walking home to his native village of Laxay, from nearby Keose, in the island of Lewis. He had reached a bridge crossing a small burn when his eyes caught sight of a strange light. Thinking it was someone from his own village with a torch, he called out but got no answer. He called out again and this time the response was a flaring of the light and its lengthening vertically to the height of a man. This time, thinking it was a friend playing some kind of trick, he called out a third time. Again there was no answer. So John went over to the light to grapple with it and was suddenly confronted by a large dark form which began to wrestle with him. Try as he might, and he was no inexperienced fighter, John was unable to come to grips with his mysterious opponent. After a time, the struggle brought him near to the edge of the burn. As he lay on the ground, with the water gurgling in his ear, he, in a last desperate attempt for his life, managed to say: 'God have mercy on me!' Instantly his opponent relaxed the hold which had kept John firmly on the ground. As he recovered John saw that he had been fighting, not flesh and blood, but a spirit form. Then, forced by the ghost's overpowering presence, he was persuaded to sit on the bridge wall to hear what the ghost had to say.

The latter had once been a drover from the Scottish mainland who, some years previously, had visited Lewis to buy cattle. With this end in view, he had gone to Laxay to look at some beasts. There he met up with a local man who, suspecting that the drover carried a good purseful of money, set upon him at a spot close by and murdered him. He robbed the body before burying it beside the burn where the present bridge was erected a few years later. The drover's body was never found and the murderer and gone free and unpunished. The ghost said, however, that the gables of the house in which the murderer's family still lived could be seen from the bridge, and that the murderer's lineal descendant had since left the village to take up work on the Scottish mainland.

After his encounter, and his release by the ghost, John managed to make his way home where he alarmed his relatives, who were anxiously waiting up for him, by becoming violently sick. He was confined to his bed for a week with an illness which defied the local doctor's attempt to diagnose and treat. While this story may seem to mirror other tales about encounters with the ghosts of murdered pedlars and similar itinerants, the family of John (a fictitious name) still lives in the neighbouring village of Keose and the encounter tended to confirm local suspicions about the murder, and the murderer's family.

Over the years, many of the grimmest incidents in Highland history have acquired an aura of romance—the result of the original details being clothed in a fashion more suitable for telling at *ceilidhs* and for passing on by folktale bearers and others. One such incident concerns the notorious Assynt murder, for which Hugh MacLeod, Lynneanach, was publicly hanged at the Longman, Inverness, in 1831—and all because that peculiar Highland gift of second sight was involved in the solving of the crime and was instrumental in bringing justice to its rightful quarter.

Indeed, one of the chief reasons why this murder is remembered is because of its association with Fraser the Dreamer. Many people over the past 150 years or so have believed that it was a dream which brought MacLeod to court and justice, conviction and death. In fact, though MacLeod's dream did produce material evidence and caused the trial to be postponed for six months, it is more than probable that MacLeold's behaviour, plus the heavy weight of circumstantial evidence, would have resulted in conviction, even if Fraser had not entered the affair at all.

Hugh MacLeod, the chief personality in the crime, was a strange character, tortured in his mind; the crime he committed was crude and brutal. Yet, there are indications in his evidence that he was not entirely responsible for his deed. His childhood was that of a precocious child who disappointed his parents. His father, Roderick MacLeod, was a pious and industrious crofter who, despite poverty, did his best to bring up his son with a respect for God and man, and tried as best he could to provide Hugh with a good education. The boy was well noted for his gentleness and consideration for others; indeed, it seemed that his father's high hopes for him and a good future were well founded.

Unfortunately, the heavy hand of grim poverty in which the Mac-Leod family lived, brought Hugh's education to an end at the age of ten. He had to go out to work and gradually consorting with rough company, he fell into their habits and developed into a hard drinker and an inveterate gambler. As he grew older he acquired a passion for being a dandy, and was often to be seen sporting himself at balls and dances. As he himself said in a letter to Mr Davidson, a schoolmaster who later was to visit him in prison: "I gave myself over to the whisky and had great pleasure in deceiving women. I forgot my father's business entirely and put the fear of God and man behind me."

Even so, incredible though it might seem today, at the age of sixteen he managed to get a job as a schoolmaster at Coigach Lochbroom; but in his continual desire to cut a fine figure he ran up debts and trouble clouds gathered thick and fast around him. His first theft was a petty one: an article of clothing from a merchant in Lochbroom. The deed was not discovered. But a later theft of a few shillings from the house of two old ladies, while they were at church, was found out and, in shame and remorse, MacLeod took to heavy drinking.

MacLeod said that, when sober, he could never think of any way of paying his increasing debts; but he was never lost for ideas when in his cups. His debts weighed heavily on his mind and he went to great pains to hide them from his parents. He told Mr Davidson, the visiting schoolmaster, that at one time he had thought that if he could get clear of debt, he could become a respectable person. But he could not raise the money and he realized that for him respectability was an impossible attainment.

Then a grim solution presented itself to him, in the form of Murdoch Grant, a travelling pedlar.

"I watched the pedlar all Thursday," he said, "for the purpose of taking away his life and robbing him. I slung my father's mason

hammer, the handle of which I shortened for the sake of conveni-
ence, in below my great coat. I knew where he had to pass and I
got into a hole where I could see all without being seen."

When the pedlar came in sight MacLeod hailed him with every
appearance of friendship and, on the pretext of wishing to buy
something, induced him to go back the way he had just come. At
times he even carried the pedlar's pack for him, but was afraid to
strike him for fear of being seen. Suddenly, near a loch, he turned
and felled the pedlar with a terriffic blow to the ear. Grant fell at
once. "He lay sprawling in great agony but never spoke. I took the
money from his warm pocket and put it into mine. There was
about £9. I gave him two or three violent blows and dragged the
body into the loch as far as I could with safety to myself."

The body would not stay down, so MacLeod got a large stone
and placed it on the dead man's chest; he threw the hammer into
the loch and then rifled the pack. "I took the most portable things
such as stockings and silk handkerchiefs and sunk the heavy goods
into a moss loch farther into the moors."

From then on MacLeod lived in a private hell, which grew in
immensity as each day passed. He paid off some of his debts with
the stolen money, but he was ever haunted by the image and cries of
the pedlar and tried to drown them in drink. He saw the body day
after day as he passed close by the loch on his way to and from
work, but never plucked up enough courage to retrieve it and bury
it. Yet, so urgent was his desire to dress in finery, he went about
wearing tartan clothes from the pedlar's pack.

It was to be some six weeks after the crime that the pedlar's
body was found floating in the loch by a crofter. According to the
evidence given at the trial by one Angus MacLeod, Culcairn, there
was much blood on the body and serious wounds on the face and
head. Neighbours assisted the crofter in getting the body out of the
water after which they "bound something about it and put it back
into the loch until the next day to keep it fresh". The banks of
the loch were composed of moss and the fresh moss water had
helped to preserve the body. Mr William Ross, a surgeon, and Mr
R. H. Grant, another surgeon, said they were fully satisfied that the
pedlar was dead 'before he was committed to the water because,

had he been alive, it is most probable that a quantity of water would have been found in the stomach, which was perfectly empty'.

Suspicion immediately fell on Hugh MacLeod, partly because of the way he had been throwing money around and partly because of his strange behaviour at the pedlar's funeral. The country folk, following the age-old superstition, all went forward and touched the body, MacLeod, on the other hand, absolutely refused to go near it. He kept apart on a hill overlooking the spot in the company of some children, and when anyone looked his way he cowered and went behind a rock.

Eventually he was arrested on suspicion on 22nd September 1830, and was brought up for trial at Inverness, being taken from Dornoch, where he had been imprisoned. An entry dated 14th July 1830, in the *Inverness Courier* notes: "A daring attempt was lately made to escape from the gaol of Dornoch by Hugh MacLeod, the young man suspected of the atrocious murder at Assynt, and a convict of the name of MacDonald. The parties, we understand, arranged to seize the gaolers, take the keys, and thus effect their escape. Information was, however, conveyed to the authorities by another prisoner who had overheard the scheme, and steps were taken which prevented its completion. The prisoners were accordingly lodged in separate cells and strictly guarded."

At Inverness arrangements were made to call a jury, but when it was found that there was not sufficient special jurymen available, the trial proceedings were postponed until the following Circuit Court to be held in April 1831.

By that time fresh evidence had been received from Kenneth Fraser, called 'the Dreamer', who was employed as a tailor. Fraser had met MacLeod in the April, a fortnight after the murder and he had seen the killer with money and a red pocket-book. They had gone about together for a day or two, drinking, with MacLeod paying for everything. When Fraser was called as a witness he said that he had seen in a dream where the pedlar's pack was lying: "I was at home when I had the dream in the month of February. It was said to me in my sleep by a voice, like a man's voice, that the pack was lying in sight of the place. I got a sight of the place just as if I had been awake. I never saw the place before but the voice said in Gaelic, 'The pack of the merchant is lying in a cairn of stones in a hollow near to their house'. The voice did not name MacLeod's house. When the officer came I took him to the place I had got a sight of. It was on the south-west side of Loch Tor-na-h-eigin. We found nothing there and we then went to search on the south side of the burn. I had not seen this place in my dream but it was not far from the place I had seen in my dream that the things were found. There were five silk handkerchiefs."

The effect of this weird story told shortly after midnight, in the dimly-lit court-room, and among a class of people who believed strongly in the supernatural was 'awe-inspiring'.

When both prosecution and defence had delivered their final summing up speeches, the jury retired, to return with a verdict: "Guilty as libelled". MacLeod's reaction was to stand up in the dock and exclaim: "The Lord Almighty knows that I am innocent. I didn't think any one in this country would be condemned on mere opinion."

Then Lord Medwyn proposed the sentence which, he said, must necessarily follow the conviction and the verdict just pronounced —a conviction and verdict which were founded on the clearest evidence. His Lordship referred in affecting terms to the position of the prisoner and concluded by proposing as the sentence of the Court that the prisoner, Hugh MacLeod, should be executed on the 24th October, ensuing at Inverness between the hours of two and four in the afternoon, and that his body be given to the Professors of Anatomy in Edinburgh for dissection.

MacLeod persistently denied his guilt, but later he confessed and, as the day of his execution approached, became very calm and collected. On the night before his execution the ministers who visited him were astonished by his skill and eloquence in discussion; and on the appointed day, when the blacksmith came to strike off his irons, he showed little or no emotion, but turned very pale. When one of the magistrates asked him if he could walk to the place of execution, or whether he would prefer to go in the cart which was made ready, he replied that he could walk ten miles if necessary.

At half-past one o'clock he left the prison. A large crowd was assembled in the street, but after taking one look at them, Mac-Leod kept his eyes fixed on the Bible which he carried open in his hand. He was dressed in a long black cloak, made for the occasion, and had on a white nightcap. He was accompanied on his right by the Rev. Mr Clark, and Mr. E. Davidson, schoolmaster, and on his left by Rev. Mr Kennedy and a Mr MacKenzie, a shoemaker. The magistrates also walked in procession and the party, escorted by the Inverness Militia, and a number of constables, proceeded to the sea beach at the Longman, where the gallows was erected.

It was a cold, bleak day, similar to that on which MacLeod had killed Murdoch Grant the pedlar about eighteen months before. The large audience which had come to watch his death were not disappointed. MacLeod gave his Psalm book and Bible to one of the ministers for delivery to his parents, and then delivered an address in Gaelic and another in English; then, after shaking hands with the ministers and those around him, he knelt for a few seconds in prayer. When he ascended the drop and the executioner had pulled the cap over his face, he said part of a psalm in a loud, clear voice, before dropping his handkerchief as a sign, exclaiming twice: "The Lord receive my spirit."

Thus, at the age of twenty-two, died Hugh MacLeod, the man who was to become known in Highland folk tradition as the Assynt Murderer. The crowd of nearly 6,000, many who had come from far afield went away with the scene firmly implanted in their memories, most likely to ponder on the fate of Hugh MacLeod and to do some heart-searching of their own.

SIX

Highland Mysteries

All countries worth their historical salt abound with mysteries involving people initiating happenings and events with outcomes which have never quite been resolved, even to the present day when historical research has reached such a high peak of professional skill. Scotland is not too far down the list with her quota of mysteries ranging from the 'Casket Letters' of Mary, Queen of Scots, the Gowrie Conspiracy, the case of Daniel Douglas Home (the nineteenth-century medium), the case of Captain Green (hanged on the sands of Leith, innocent of crime), and the case of Allan Breck, implicated in the Appin Murder affair. Within Scotland's marches, the Highlands have also contributed a share of the spoils of mystery over the centuries and some are here presented. What makes this particular Highland pageant interesting is the occasional glimpse of characters, or individual members of particular clans, flitting across the stage from set to set as they fulfilled some kind of destiny to be dabblers in the affairs of men and the State; or else to see their descendants indulging in the same penchants for mystery and intrigue as, more often that not, got their forebears into trouble.

In 1758, Scotland was made aware of strange criminal practices in the Highlands which had been carried on for years with extraordinary impunity. In that year, Peter Williamson, having returned from an adventurous career among the Cherokee Indians published his life and adventures. He told how he had been kidnapped in Aberdeen when eleven years old, and had been carried off with many others to America, where he was sold to a planter for £16. Later he was captured by Indians, from whom he escaped. After a life full of adventures, he arrived back in Scotland to write his book which set the country on its heels and opened many eyes to a contemporary despicable trade in human beings which went on for some years and which involved many men who held high public position. Many lords of regality made profits by selling prisoners to agents who shipped these overseas to work in the plantations. Williamson was later brought to court as the result of 'influence in high places'. After trial he was freed and awarded £100 damages. This story of kidnapping made the public reflect on the famous case of Lady Grange which had caught Scotland's imagination only a decade previously.

Mrs Erskine of Grange was the daughter of a Mr Cheisly of Dalry, Edinburgh, a man reputed to have a violent temper and of such fiery passions that he once shot Sir George Lockhart, Lord President of the Court of Sessions, for having decided against him in a lawsuit. She was a beautiful woman. It was said that she had some hold over James Erskine of Grange and forced him to marry her. Whatever the reason, the marriage was fated from the start to be both disastrous and tragic; and so it turned out to be, affording Scotland with one of the biggest scandals of the eighteenth century and which set tongues wagging in every howf in Edinburgh and in every 'change-house' in the remotest part of the Highlands. James Erskine was made a Lord of Session in 1707 by the title of Lord Grange. His family were staunch Jacobites and this allegiance often led the Erskine family into many strange and often disastrous attachments. It wrecked not just a few noble houses of distinction in Scotland, but for many years involved the whole region of the Highlands in unjust and indiscriminate suspicion, the consequences of which also extended widely over the lowland districts of Scotland. Lord Grange died in London in 1754, aged seventy-five. He had eight children by his wife.

For many years those families disaffected to the Hanoverian succession were in the practice of holding secret meetings in Edinburgh, to plan ways and means to overthrow the Government and restore the Stuarts to the British throne. Many persons of importance, and with large personal fortunes, joined one clandestine association, among them being several clan chiefs anxious to forward the 'Cause'. Deputations from this association were frequently sent to France and Italy, and a regular correspondence was kept up with the Chevalier de St George.

Many meetings were held in Lord Grange's house; they were usually conducted in such circumstances that they began to excite the suspicions of Lady Grange, an equally staunch Hanoverian. At first she was afraid for her husband, that he might ruin both his career and his family, and she begged of him to tell her the nature and import of the meetings; but Lord Grange refused to take her into his confidence. This upset his wife and she began to fret. Lord Grange was, in any case, far from being an amiable man. In fact he was extremely dissipated, of a restless and intriguing disposition and, from the moment he was forced to marry his wife, was "not possessed of immaculate fidelity". His wife, on the other hand, was of a violent, suspicious and determined character. Her attachment to the House of Hanover was almost fanatical and the frequent visits of Highland chiefs to her house, whom she knew to be Jacobites, made her imagination work overtime. Eventually, by single-mindedness, she discovered the reasons for the meetings and luck, or ill-luck as it turned out, came her way when she actually obtained possession of some papers which gave details of a variety of plots against the Government. To confirm matters, she managed to conceal herself where she overheard the whole of a conversation her husband had with his partners, concerning the manner of arming the Highlands and, more, the place where a force from France was to be landed on the west coast.

Armed with her dangerous information, Lady Grange told her husband and began a series of remonstrations with him to persuade him to retreat from his intentions. When he refused to budge from his already deeply entrenched position, she finally threatened to disclose all she knew to the authorities. Another side to the affair was her suspicions of Lord Grange's frequent visits to London, and his amorous adventures there. Lord Grange found himself in a quandary and determined to resolve the matter as speedily as possible. He lost no time in telling his friends. Understandably they were alarmed: heads and fortunes could be lost literally at a stroke of both pen and axe.

After much earnest discussion it was agreed that the lady should

K

be secured instantly and taken as far away from Edinburgh as possible, preferably to some safe, remote and unfrequented place, where she could be concealed until such time as their mission was complete. Lord Grange, considering his new and irreversible relationship with her, agreed and plans were laid. So that he might not in reality have any hand in the kidnapping of Lady Grange, he went away from Edinburgh for a few days.

Two persons were hired for the kidnapping, and were given detailed instructions as to what they had to do; they were also given a key to get them into the house. A dark night helped the enterprise and allowed them to approach the house of Grange unseen. Once inside, they crept their way towards Lady Grange's room but were seen by a servant who raised a hue and cry. Shouts of alarm rang through the house, lights were struck and a gun was fired; the two men barely escaped with their lives. When Lord Grange returned from his 'holiday' he was furious to learn that his wife was still free and in Edinburgh and that the mission had failed. This failure made him resolve to get rid of his wife by whatever means he could think of. It was still, however, as essential as ever to keep her away from the authorities. He refused after the incident to live in his house and took lodgings in Edinburgh with his children. Some time later he proposed a legal separation, but this was refused by Lady Grange who now knew the extent of her husband's hatred of her. She, too, took lodgings in the city, but after a while she resolved to leave Scotland and reside permanently in London. This intention was discussed by Lord Grange who lost no time in laying plans for another attempt at abduction.

Included in the plans was Margaret MacLean, who owned the house where Lady Grange lodged. Her part in the plot was fulfilled when she arranged for her servants to be off to their beds long before the usual time and had the maidservant, who attended on Lady Grange, also sent out of the way. Two men were appointed to conduct the business: MacDonald of Morar and a brother of the Laird of MacLeod of Skye. But the chief engineer of the scheme was Fraser of Lovat.

About 11 p.m. on the night of 22nd April 1732, MacDonald and MacLeod, accompanied by several of their henchmen, knocked at the door of Margaret MacLean's house. They were admitted and they went straight to Lady Grange's room. When challenged they told her that it was their intention to remove her, for her own good, from Edinburgh. A letter from her husband was read out, in which she was asked to co-operate and to go quietly with the men who would move her to more comfortable lodgings. But she resisted. Then, exasperated by the situation, the men moved in and in a short time the terrified woman was wound in a sheet, tied and gagged and bundled into a sedan waiting at the front door of the house. On the outskirts of the city she was transferred to a horse and taken to Linlithgow, where the party went into hiding in the house of a lawyer named MacLeod, a zealous Jacobite.

By the nightfall of the next day the party was on the move again. Arriving at Polmaise, near Falkirk, Lady Grange was held captive there until 15th August, when she was told to prepare herself for another journey. This time the party went to Stirling, where they crossed the Forth, and trekked towards Callander, where the night was spent in a house with a room which had been specially prepared for her. The next day MacDonald appeared to tell her that they had had her care devolved on himself and MacLeod. He assured her that all her trouble was for her own good and, indeed, was partly to keep her out of the hands of her husband who had by now the utmost hatred of her. This latter reason was no doubt partly true, for any misdeed perpetrated by Lord Grange on his lady would have rebounded on his associates whose plans would then have been made public. The real danger was that her death would involve Lord Grange and the consequences would lead to the probable death of them all.

Tracks began once more on the following day towards the Highlands. It was difficult work: bogs, hills, rivers to cross, all made the journey trying for the party; and the need to be constantly on the alert for Highland brigands added to their troubles. They stayed the night at a place near Balquhidder, where their appearance roused some suspicion. The castle-type building was, in fact, an old keep of the Macgregors and was used as a hideout for an un-principled band of robbers.

The latter were doubtful about the newcomers whom they

suspected of being spies, notwithstanding the fact that there was a woman in the party, whose presence was explained away as being a patient in need of the curing properties of St Fillan's Well, which had the reputation of being able to effect miraculous cures of cases of mental illness. MacLeod, with his knowledge of Gaelic, managed to overhear himself and his party made the subject of some debate among the robbers. Some wanted to kill the strangers; others, presumably reflecting the ancient respect for the old code of Highland hospitality and the plight of strangers in need of shelter, were against this. Eventually it was agreed to leave the strangers alone but to keep them under close observation until they were found innocent of spying. During the night, the leader of the outlaw band, a Buchanan of Machar, who had wondered about the situation of a lady of quality touring the Highlands in the company of armed guards, found his way to Lady Grange's room to ask the truth of her situation. He was not in fact a common bandit by vocation. Rather he had fallen on hard times, the result of several lawsuits, and had been deprived of his lands by neighbours, and in order to be revenged had associated with the gang of ruffians to become their leader. Two of Rob Roy Macgregor's sons originally belonged to this band but now they only went on expeditions with them when the pickings were large and worthwhile. To Lady Grange, Buchanan was a saviour. When she told him the whole story, Buchanan saw a chance to put some reward money in the hands of his companions and, possibly, a chance to gain the respect of the law for his deed if he informed the authorities, with the aim of securing his former properties again.

He informed his companions of the matter who agreed to set Lady Grange free and to restrain her escort. But while they talked, they were overheard by two Fraser henchmen in MacDonald's party, who at once informed the latter. Thus forewarned, the abducting party prepared for battle—but nothing happened. The weather had in any case turned atrocious and all in the old keep were in no way inclined to journey outside.

Towards nightfall, by a strategy, the four escorts found themselves locked in a room by the brigands; but a door yielded to their combined efforts and they were freed to overpower a guard set by the bandits at the door of Lady Grange's room. They woke up the poor woman and told her to get her things ready for leaving. Shortly afterwards the party managed to escape from the keep and, with as much speed as they could muster, made towards the west arriving, after a terrible journey, at Glencoe where they rested at the inn. Then it was on again to Glenfinnan and Loch Shiel to Castle Tiorram, in Ardnamurchan, which was to be Lady Grange's prison for some weeks. By this time Lady Grange's health had deteriorated and at one time was in the firm clutches of a fever, from which she made a recovery of sorts.

Her stay at Castle Tiorram was short, for she found herself on a sloop chartered to take her to the Hebrides; the ship was commanded by Alexander MacDonald of Sleat in Skye. Eventually, after a voyage fated to be beset by storms, Heisgeir Island was reached (the Monach Isles off Uist), where she was kept until May 1734 when she was once again told she was to be shifted because rumours on the Scottish mainland indicated that she was being hidden away on the Uists. So, on 14th June, a sloop arrived off-shore, with a letter from the Laird of MacLeod, with instructions to the ship's master that the poor much-travelled woman was to be removed to St Kilda, a group of islands some forty or so miles out into the deep Atlantic Ocean.

She was eventually landed on St Kilda and left in the charge of a man who spoke very bad English; her home was a rude hut furnished with nothing but bare essentials and thatched with local heather and grass. At first the islanders paid her no attention, but after some months her plight attracted some sympathy and her life was made a little easier—which was just as well for her stay on St Kilda was to last nearly a decade.

Many years passed in confinement until she found an opportunity of hiding a couple of letters in balls of island yarn destined for sale on the mainland. These letters found their way to the addressee, an old friend in Edinburgh who immediately took steps to secure her release. But before this could happen she was moved off St Kilda and taken to Assynt on the west coast of northern Scotland. From there she was taken on a final escorted journey to Skye where she endured so much harsh treatment that she was allowed to wander about the place at will, having completely lost her mind. In this state she lived for a few more years until she died. But even in death she was not left in peace: she was buried in the cemetery at Trumpan in Waternish, while a mock funeral was held at Dunvegan where a coffin filled with sods and stones was duly interred with great ceremony.

After Culloden had been lost by the Jacobites, Murlaggan, at the head of Loch Arkaig, was chosen as a meeting-place of the chiefs, convened for the purpose of determining whether or not hostilities should be continued. Though he had been severely wounded, Cameron of Lochiel was present, accompanied by his brother, Dr Archibald Cameron. Among others who attended were Lord Lovat, the young Chief of Clanranald, Glenbucket, MacDonald of Barrisdale, John Roy Stewart, Alexander MacLeod of Neuck, MacDonald, a nephew of Keppoch, and the Laird of MacKinnon. The conference decided that the struggle should not be abandoned, little knowing that the Duke of Cumberland was creating a desert of many parts of the Highlands. Accordingly, the respective chiefs undertook to muster the remnants of their clans, and agreed to meet in council at Achnacarry in Lochaber on a future date. But Cumberland had meantime issued peremptory orders to the Earl of Loudon, instructing him to proceed at once to Lochaber with an army of 1,700 men, with a view to nip in the bud any attempt at further rebellion. Intelligence of this move was conveyed to Cameron of Lochiel just in time to prevent his capture, and the presence in the country of Loudon's militia nullified the efforts of the chiefs to bring about a second rising.

A little below where the River Arkaig flows out of Loch Arkaig, the beautiful Falls of Kaig are well worth a visit. The loch itself reaches some ten miles into the very heart of the great rampart of mountains that girdles the west coast of Scotland. The loch has an interest of its own, altogether apart from its scenic splendour. On 8th May 1746 two French vessels touched at Borrodale. They carried seven barrels of gold—37,000 *louis d'or*—from the King of France, to assist the ill-fated Forty-five. After landing the money, the sailors heard of the desperate condition of the enterprise— Culloden had been fought and lost only three weeks previously—

and demanded the restoration of the gold. They landed a party to recover the barrels, but all was to no avail and when three English ships appeared off the coast, the French vessels had to forsake their quest and fight their way out to the open sea.

The English ships were anxious to secure their prize and, under the command of Captain Howe, managed to manœuvre in between the Frenchmen to fire a broadside at each. He succeeded in temporarily disabling the larger of the two, but towards evening the damage had been repaired and the fight was resumed to last for twelve hours. By this time Howe's ships were running short of ammunition and he was forced to set sail, with the French frigates on his tail. The bodies of fifteen Frenchmen were afterwards found on the shores; the English did not cast off their dead until passing the Point of Ardnamurchan. The sea battle was watched by groups of country folk and the scene is still lodged in local tradition.

In the meantime, the treasure was carried by Highlanders to the head of Loch Arkaig, where the council of war, referred to above, was held. With the English soldiers scouring the country far and wide, it was impossible to carry the gold from place to place; so enough was removed to relieve immediate wants, and the rest was buried, part in the little river that runs in at the head of the loch, with the remainder near the lower end of the same loch. In the bed of the small burn opposite Murlaggan three barrels containing 15,000 *louis d'or* were deposited. Later the treasure was dug up again and reburied, but subsequent searches failed to reveal the place of concealment. A very considerable part of the gold has never yet been accounted for, though many entertain doubt on this subject. *Sporrain ghobhlach do dh'or a' Phrionnsa* (Forked purses of the Prince's gold) is a local epithet applied to those who acquire wealth by unknown methods, the inference being that the party referred to must have chanced upon some of the hidden treasure, now part of the mystery of Loch Arkaig. It was once reported, at the turn of this century, that one man did discover some at least of the long-lost treasure; but it is more than possible that a rich find yet remains to be upturned by an enterprising and intelligent seeker.

One day in the year 1880, the S.S. *Ferret* failed to make her home pier at Stromeferry in Wester Ross, and the incident occupied the attention of many for the following couple of years, not only in the Highlands but all over the world, thereby earning the *Ferret* a place in the spectrum of Highland mysteries. The S.S. *Ferret* was owned by the Highland Railway Company. A coaster of 346 tons, she was fitted out for sailings in the stormy waters of the Minch and the Inner Sound. She was normally based at Stromeferry where she handled cargoes brought this far north on their journey to Skye and the Outer Isles. Then, on a day which dawned as uneventful as many others, in June 1880, she sailed from the Clyde and disappeared without trace. Despite cabled messages from her owners, and worried consultation with her insurers' agents in all ports all over the country, she disappeared more or less from human ken. It was a mystery which, at the time, was placed beside that of the *Marie Celeste* and other strange mysteries of the open sea.

Then, in June 1881, readers of the London *Times* and the *Glasgow Herald* were informed by Reuter's telegram, sent nearly four weeks previously, that the steamer had been discovered in far-off Melbourne, in Australia—just about as far as she could have sailed from her home port. The message read: "The reputed owner, the captain, and the purser of the steamer *India*, alias *Ferret*, have been arrested on a charge of forging the ship's register, and have been re-manded. The discovery of a telegraphic code on board the vessel leads to the belief that there were accomplices in England, concerned with the fraud."

The details of the story were eventually sent half way round the world to satisfy the readers of these newspapers. A police constable, a native of Wester Ross, who had emigrated to Australia and, as is the case with emigrant Scots, had kept up his contacts with home, received a number of Glasgow papers in which he read of the mysterious disappearance of the *Ferret*. He was also familiar with the ship's outline, build and appearance, having seen her often at the pier at Stromeferry. When he saw the *India* steaming quietly into Melbourne, he was struck by her resemblance to the *Ferret*. His curiosity got the better of him and he went to the Head of the Port Customs and searched through Lloyd's Register, but found no entry for a ship of the size under the given name. But it was described perfectly under the entry for the long-lost *Ferret*. The police were informed at once and a party of constables and armed marines boarded the ship and arrested the crew; then the *India* was moored alongside the warship *Cerberus*, so that she could not escape to sea again.

The ringleaders were Captain Wright, alias Carlton, William Wallace, alias Walker, the Purser, and an enterprising and ingenious character variously known as Henderson and Smith, posing as the owner of the *India*. It transpired, on close investigation, that the hi-jacking of the *Ferret* was not carried out on the spur of the moment, nor was it intended as a short-term adventure. On board the ship were all kinds of forged documents and official stamps, even to the extent of a small printing press for producing bogus bills of lading, and a fair supply of arms and ammunition. Most damaging of all among the evidence found was a special telegraph code book, obviously designed for sending secret messages back to mysterious agents in Britain. The codes themselves were more than incriminating:

"Everything wrong. No one contented. Dangerous."
"Vessel seized. Everything U.P. Could destroy nothing."
"Destroy everything and be onguard. Failure."
"Lloyd's agents will call to make enquiries. Be prepared as previously agreed upon."
"Game is up; all discovered; destroy or hide everything, and make yourself scarce. Communicate with me through the arranged channel."

The ordinary crew members, after questioning, revealed that they were unaware of what was going on and, indeed, the code book contained rather sinister entries implying that members of the crew might have had to be disposed of summarily if things came out into the open prematurely.

It took some time to piece together how the *Ferret* got half way round the world; and then parts of the story were never told, to remain only a partially-solved mystery of the sea. The *Ferret* had been stolen when she was in the Clyde, taken to Greenock, then on to Cardiff for coal and a new crew. After bunkering, she sailed through the Bay of Biscay towards Gibraltar. Here some comical turns took place. Rather than steam into harbour, she passed within a couple of cable-lengths with a board which prominently displayed her original name pointed towards the docks. Then she went into the Mediterranean Sea; but as soon as darkness fell, she turned about and sailed out into the Atlantic, with all lights doused. This manœuvre was intended to trap expected pursuers into thinking that she had made for the Suez Canal.

Anderson and Wright then took the *Ferret* across the Atlantic in easy stages to Santos in Brazil, having changed her name to the *Benton* in the meantime. At Santos they picked up coal and a cargo of coffee for Cape Town. But only a few days off the Cape she ran out of coal and several hundred bags of coffee were burned in the boilers for steam to keep the ship going. With the reduced cargo, Henderson sold the coffee for more than £10,000, of which sum he got £2,000, with the remainder of £8,000 in bills of exchange sent to a mysterious principal in London. The *Benton* then sailed on into the Indian Ocean, to try unsuccessfully for a cargo of sugar at Mauritius and finally arrived at Melbourne under the name of the *India*. There, because of the failure to secure a cargo at Mauritius, Henderson tried to sell the ship. He was offered £8,500, but he stuck out for £10,000. His crew were busy freshening up the *India* paintwork when the police arrived. Had Henderson accepted the original offer of £8,500 he might well have escaped with the loot. Instead, the purser and the captain were tried, found guilty and each sentenced to seven years' penal servitude. As for the *Ferret*, she never saw her home base again at Stromeferry. She was kept in Australian waters until she was wrecked in a storm in 1920.

The Flannan Isles lie in a close group of Atlantic outliers about twenty miles west by north from Gallan Head on the west coast of Lewis. The group contains seven islands worthy of the name and a number of small islets, rocks and reefs. There are three subgroups. To the north are Eilean Mor and Eilean Tighe. To the south and west are the smaller islands. The Flannans are part of the civil Parish of Uig in Lewis. The islands are remarkable for the manner in which they rise sheer from the sea. The largest is Eilean Mor (Big

Island) which has a maximum height of 288 feet above sea level. The largest islands in the group have grassy tops and all support a large number of seabirds. The Flannans are a favourite haunt of the grey seal, though it does not breed among the islands.

The cliffs on the island are so steep that landing is always extremely difficult and hazardous, and is only possible when the weather is favourable. For the swell of the Atlantic waters can easily smash a small boat against the hard and unrelenting rockfaces. Landing on Eilean Mor is from two places: the east and south landings. These are built up from concrete blocks placed and cemented against the cliffs. When the weather does not permit an actual boat landing, cranes above each landing-place take stores and sometimes men ashore to the now-unattended lighthouse.

The Flannans Light is one of a chain of lights in the western approaches of the Atlantic. The lighthouse was built between 1895 and 1899 by D. and C. Stevenson of Edinburgh, the firm of which Robert Louis Stevenson's father was the head. The tower is 75 feet high, to make the light stand about 330 feet above sea level. It was first lit on 7th December 1899. The light on Eilean Mor is one of the most remote lighthouses and was, until recently, served by four men.

For centuries the sea has been the sole possessor of clues to the many unsolved mysteries, strange happenings, baffling phenomena which have taken place on the surface of its waters. On a par with the mystery of the *Marie Celeste*, the complete and utter disappearance of three keepers from the lighthouse on Eilean Mor in December 1900 has been, and still is, a matter for new theories to account for the happening.

On 15th December 1900, the steamer *Archer*, bound from Philadelphia to Leith, passed within a few miles of the island group. Though the black masses of the islands were clearly visible in the moonlight, there was no beam of light from the lantern on Eilean Mor. The skipper of the *Archer* reported his discovery when he made a landing at Oban. A message was sent to the Scottish Lighthouse Board relief ship *Hesperus*, which was anchored in Little Loch Roag, on the west of Lewis. But before she could venture out to investigate the incident, a series of strong gales blew up and it was not until the 26th December that she was able to make steam for the Flannans.

When the *Hesperus* reached the island group she signalled her arrival by whistle, then by rocket. From her position at the east landing her crew could see the lighthouse buildings. But there was no flag signal from the flagstaff, nor were there the usual signs of activity which accompanied the arrival of a ship. A boat was lowered and a party went ashore. At the jetty, the first sign was noticed that something was amiss. Normally, it would have been piled high with empty provision boxes for return to the shore base on Lewis. Now it was bare.

In a mounting fit of alarm, the party, which included Joseph Moore, a relief keeper, climbed up the concrete steps and ran up over the inclined path over the brow of the cliff to the lighthouse. There was an uncanny silence which was accentuated when they entered the living-room. The fire was dead. The clock had stopped. On the table lay a meal which had never been touched. There was cold meat, pickles and a dish of potatoes. An overturned chair lay a silent witness on the floor. The men then went up the spiral steps to the sleeping quarters. There they found the beds, made up in the clean, clinical way of sailors. In the galley pots, pans and dishes sparkled. Moore went up to the lantern room to find the lamp cold. The wicks had been trimmed and the lenses were polished clean. All was operational in fact. There was absolutely no reason for the lamp being out.

After a further search the logbook of the chief keeper, Ducat, was found with entries made up to 13th December. A slate was discovered which took the record to 09.00 hours on the morning of 15th December. The entries told of weather conditions and the state of the lantern. The log reported that there had been gales and heavy seas for a week and there was evidence of severe damage at the west landing which had been reduced to a shambles. A crane, which had been set fast in a bed of concrete some one hundred feet above the high-water mark, had been torn from its fixings. A concrete rope box about forty feet higher up had also been torn away and smashed to pieces. Heavy iron stanchions on the concrete stairs were found to be twisted. And for about thirty feet along the top of the cliff, standing some 200 feet above high-water mark, the turf had been torn away. A boulder weighing nearly a ton had been wrested from its centuries-old bed and rolled a considerable distance.

Obviously the storm had been unusually severe. But the keepers had survived it and the last entry on the slate made by Principal Ducat was that the wind was moderating. A search carried on out-side the lighthouse revealed no sign of the keepers. Nothing was found which could account for the disappearance of the three men. The mystery was heightened by the fact that Ducat's and Marshall's oilskins and Wellington boots were missing. Only Mac-Arthur's clothes and boots could be found.

A full-scale investigation was begun. Some facts emerged from the enquiry. One was that the oilskins and seaboots were used by the keepers only when visiting one or other of the landings. The other was that the east landing was in good repair while that on the west side of the island was in bad need of reconstruction and repair. In the end, no definite conclusion was reached as to the ex-planation of the disappearance of the three men. "It is to be as-sumed," said the official report, "that the three men, for some reason, left their post, were caught by an unexpected heavy sea and drowned."

The nearest explanation of the mystery comes from local know-ledge of the sea conditions which sometimes exist round the Flan-nans, which conditions it would not be expected men on Eilean Mor to know in their first year on the island. The theory also accounts for the damage done to the west landing. After severe storms in the Atlantic, huge isolated waves come rolling in on the islands to dash against the rock-cliffs. The rebound waves are often more violent than the original or parent wave. The west landing on Eilean Mor is in an inlet called Skipigeo. It is a few hundred yards long and ends in a cave. At high tide this cave can be completely closed. In certain conditions of high storm, wave upon wave of water is pushed into the cave. The pressure of the resident air is thus built up to such a value that it eventually explodes out-wards and tons of water fall onto the adjacent sides of the geo, including the west jetty.

The theory about the Flannans mystery is that after the storm damage to the west landing gear, two of the keepers, Ducat and Marshall, went down to the landing wearing their outdoor clothes and boots. As they were experienced seamen they well knew to keep an eye to seawards for incoming waves. One such wave might well have swept into the geo, followed by smaller waves to begin the build-up of pressure inside the cave at the end of the geo. In the meantime, MacArthur, the third keeper, was probably in the lighthouse and setting the last touches to the breakfast table. A glance out to sea would be sufficient to notice an incoming wave of more than usual height making for the west of the island, with its attendant follower waves. Being a local man, he realized the importance of warning his mates. He rushed to the door, knocking over a chair and, forsaking his oilskins and boots, ran to the west landing calling out to watch for the wave which would rebound on the keepers below. He then might well have had to descend to the jetty to make himself understood and in the meantime died with his fellow keepers as the Skipigeo cave exploded to disgorge its death-wall of sea water onto the unfortunate men.

It will never be known for certain just what happened. One can in these matters come as close to the truth as the human imagination will allow. But the mystery still remains unsolved, like a haunting, unexorcised cloud hovering over the Flannan Islands. One cannot visit Eilean Mor, look far-down at the heaving, white-capped waves beneath and not feel that little bit unnerved at something which lies just outside the pale of human knowledge and understanding.

The total destruction of H.M.S. *Natal* on 30th December 1915, is still talked about in the port of Invergordon and the small fishing villages dotted round the shores of the Cromarty Firth in Ross-shire. The ship suffered a calamitous explosion which sent her to the bottom of the sea in a matter of minutes and which has never been fully explained to this day. Some years ago, as the result of oil-related industrial developments at Invergordon, the decision was made to remove the wreck of the *Natal*. For many years after the disaster the keel of the ship was clearly visible at low water then, as she settled on the bottom and began to disintegrate, the wreck disappeared from view. But of course she was still there: a steel carcase nearly 600 feet long, not only an obstruction to ships navigating in the Firth, put a potential explosive hazard, because she had been a fighting ship at the time of her destruction and there was a war on. Though she did not die in the face of the enemy, she was fully armed and ready to sail into battle at very short notice on that sombre December day. The salvaging operations took some months to clear away the untidy heap of twisted armour that was once the *Natal*; the metal was shipped south in railway trucks to Scottish steelworks for re-cycling and possibly to reappear in the form of a modern ship once more.

The *Natal* was an armoured cruiser of nearly 14,000 tons, launched at Barrow-in-Furness in October 1905 at a cost of £1.2 million. She was one of several vessels of her class stationed in the Cromarty Firth during the First World War while Britain's battleships lay at Scapa Flow and battle cruisers lay at Rosyth, in the Firth of Forth. The whole fleet formed what was called the Grand Fleet under the command of Sir John Jellicoe; it was reckoned to be the greatest expression of sea power the world was ever likely to see.

The 30th December 1915 was a dreich day. The war in Europe had been progressing for over a year, with no fulfilment of the initial hopes that the hostilities might last a few months only. Lives were being lost in their thousands on both land and sea in the war zones; little thought was given to the possibility that lives would also be lost off the home shores. The disaster of the *Natal* came unexpectedly. One moment the great ship took up more than its share of the seascape; the next saw a flash and flames, followed by black smoke from the explosion. Many witnessed the explosion; many more heard the effect and felt the shattering of the air in towns and villages and in remote crofts many miles from the scene. According to a story which has passed into local lore, the sailors were holding a Christmas party for children on board when the ship blew up. But on investigation this story holds little water for few if any civilians were on the ship at the time and certainly no children. What is certain is that the captain was entertaining a number of guests—some local people and several nurses from a

naval hospital ship among them—and there was to have been a
cinema show while the marine band was in attendance. Most of
those gathered in the captain's quarters lost their lives as did more
than half the ship's company of 850 officers and ratings. They were
killed by the blast, and drowned and entombed in the belly of the
ship which turned over and sank almost immediately. Of the sailors
whose bodies were recovered, some lie in the naval cemetery on
the hill above Cromarty from which the grave of their old ship
could clearly be seen.

The announcement by the Secretary of Admiralty was quite
bald: "Friday 31 December 1915. His Majesty's Ship *Natal* (Captain Eric P. Back, R.N.), armoured cruiser, sank yesterday afternoon while in harbour as the result of an internal explosion. About
400 survivors are reported, and their names are being communi-
cated to the Press as soon as possible."

One local man recalls the event:

> I remember the episode very well. I was very young at the time,
> having only just been in school a short period, but I shall never
> forget the shattering event which had such a profound effect on the
> Highland area. The explosion was heard all over the east coast of
> Ross and Sutherland, and many people in and around Invergordon
> were literally knocked off their feet. It was believed that Admiral
> Jellicoe had recently visited the ship and it was rumoured at the time
> that the enemy were after the Admiral, but their plans misfired.
> Sabotage was not ruled out, but nothing of the sort was ever proved.
> The ship's football team were lucky. At the time they were ashore
> at Invergordon playing a match. I remember seeing the wreck of
> that fine ship off Invergordon in 1924 and I believe that even later
> part of her keel continued to be seen as the ship had turned turtle
> when the magazine blew up.

It is almost certain that had the *Natal* survived until 31st May
1916, she would have taken part in the Battle of Jutland, the only
major event engagement between the main British and German
fleets during the First World War. That immense battle ended in
stalemate, the British claiming a moral victory in that the enemy
never again sought a fleet action with them. But British losses in
men and ships were immeasurably greater and among the casual-
ties were at least three of the sister ships of the *Natal*: the

Defence, the *Warrior* and the *Black Prince*. A few days after Jutland, H.M.S. *Hampshire*, another armoured cruiser was sunk by a mine off Orkney and among those who died in her was Lord Kitchener, who was travelling on a mission to Russia.

The mystery of the explosion on the *Natal*, during her last hours as a ship of the British fleet remains unexplained and is unlikely to be solved. There was a story that a U-boat had got into the Firth and torpedoed the cruiser, but this has been discounted. Only two possible explanations are left: accident or sabotage, with the former the more likely. In the previous year H.M.S. *Bulwark* was blown up in Sheerness Harbour by an internal magazine explosion; nearly 800 men perished. And in May 1915 H.M. Auxiliary Ship *Princess Irene* was also accidentally blown up in Sheerness Harbour, with the loss of many lives.

So, like H.M.S. *Bulwark* and H.M.S. *Vanguard* at Scapa Flow, destroyed, in similar circumstances and with terrible loss of life during the same war, H.M.S. *Natal* took her fatal secret with her to her watery grave.

The Duke of Kent, fourth son of King George V, was born in 1902. As a young man he had spent ten years in the Royal Navy. Artistic and somewhat unconventional, he was quite different in outlook and temperament from his brothers. The summer of 1939 found him preparing to leave England to take up the post of Governor-General of Australia. But when war was announced he put in a spell on Intelligence duties at the Admiralty; then he transferred to the Royal Air Force, relinquishing his honorary rank of Air Vice-Marshal at his own request so that he could fill a post of Group Captain in the newly-formed Welfare Branch. Touring RAF stations at home, he would often arrive without ceremony, unannounced and sometimes even unrecognized driving his own car. In 1941 he flew to Canada to see the Empire Training Scheme at work, becoming the only member of the Royal Family to cross the Atlantic both ways in a bomber. On 4th August 1942 his son, the month-old Prince Michael was christened at St Peter's, Iver. Then, after three weeks' leave, the Duke was off on another overseas welfare tour, this time to Iceland.

Beginning his journey, the Duke drove to Euston Station in

L

London, where he was joined by his private secretary and others scheduled to make the trip to Iceland with him. The train then left Euston for Inverness. Meanwhile, at about 15.30 hours on the previous afternoon, a Sunderland flying-boat of No 228 Squadron had left its base at Oban on the west coast of Scotland to fly across Inverness-shire to Invergordon, the naval base on the protected inlet of the Cromarty Firth. The crew of the plane knew that something special was 'on'; it was not until the evening of the 24th, when the Duke of Kent and his party arrived at Invergordon that they learned who their passengers were to be. Invergordon had been chosen for the rendezvous because it was the most accessible of the flying-boat bases by rail from London. The Sunderland pilot, Flight-Lieutenant Frank Goyen, was a twenty-five-year-old Australian of exceptional ability; he had been specially chosen with nearly 1,000 operational hours to his credit. With him, he had his regular crew, all equally trusted and competent. They numbered ten in all, and included a second pilot, two radio operators, three gunners, a navigator, an engineer and a fitter.

Tuesday 25th was a wet August day, with almost continuous rain. The previous fine weather had broken and storms and low cloud covered Northern Scotland; but the weather was not regarded as being bad enough to postpone the Duke's flight. Cromarty Firth was clear, the cloud-base being about 800 feet, and the forecast for the Faroes, which the Sunderland would fly over *en route* for Iceland, was that the weather was improving. At half-past twelve the aircraft crew gathered to prepare their aircraft. The flight to Iceland, a distance of nearly 900 miles, would take about seven hours. The aircraft was a Mark III Sunderland. The cruising speed was about 120 knots. Facing a long sea crossing, with the possibility of returning to base in Scotland, the aircraft had a full load of fuel. In addition to the fifteen people on board, the Sunderland carried depth charges in case submarines were seen *en route*. Because of the heavy load it was not intended that the Sunderland should turn at once on a direct course for Iceland. That would mean crossing the fringe of the north-west Highlands, where there was much high ground, with several spot heights above

3,000 feet. The climbing rate of a fully-loaded Sunderland was not quite good enough for that. Goyen, the pilot, had been briefed to follow the coastline in a north-easterly direction for eighty-five miles, keeping out to sea, before turning to port off John o' Groats to pass through the Pentland Firth, south of the Orkneys. From this point, course would be set for Iceland.

At the mouth of the Cromarty Firth estuary, Goyen turned forty-five degrees to port and began the coast crawl north-east-wards, climbing as he went. The only slight problem was that the cloud base was lowering. At first the problem was overcome by descending so that the sea's surface could be seen below the plane, and also the coastline on the left. But as they flew farther north the cloud base was lowering still further and the plane had to descend through dense banks of cloud to maintain visual contact with both sea and land. But, though the Sunderland was still over the sea, in fact the plane was drifting in towards the coast at an angle, and on its course would cross the coast-line a mile or so north of the Sutherland–Caithness border. Inland there was much high ground. The pilot, evidently satisfied that he was still over the sea, kept on descending. But directly ahead was a sharp emin-ence 900 feet high known locally as Eagle's Rock. At its present height the Sunderland would just clear it. But even the hillsides below Eagle's Rock were shrouded in mist. Two men on the ground, rounding up their sheep, heard the roar of aircraft engines. Though they looked up they could not see the plane. They heard it pass overhead. The undulating heights of the ground below were now causing considerable turbulence in the Sunderland. An up-current of air cushioned the Sunderland as it passed narrowly clear of the peak of Eagle's Rock. Then a precipitous down-draught followed. On the far side of the rock summit was a rounded shoulder, 800 feet high, towards which the aircraft was thrown. Though the impact was no more than a glancing blow, the Sunderland was racked with a violent shuddering. It ricocheted into the air, turned over uncontrollably on its back, and crashed with a terrific force 100 yards away into the heather, scoring and scorching the ground for nearly 200 yards and breaking up as it went. All but one on board were killed almost instantly. The shepherds heard the double crash and then the sudden silence of the plane's engines. It was obvious to them that the plane had crashed into high ground. But they could only guess at its position. One of them, young Hugh Morrison, ran down the sloping hillside to a stony track at the bottom, where he had left his motor bike. He drove at speed to the nearest village of Berriedale to get help. On the way he alerted estate workers, crofters and shepherds; in Berriedale the police and local doctor were contacted. For the rest of the day the volunteer searchers scoured the high ground, but thick mist and oncoming darkness forced them to give up the search. On the following day the search was resumed, and about midday they saw pieces of shattered wreckage glinting below the high shoulder of Eagle's Rock. The flying-boat had shattered into hundreds of pieces which were scattered all over the moor. Strewn around the wreckage were eleven bodies. Some little distance away was the body of a man with the ring of an air commodore on the sleeve of his uniform: the first son of a British sovereign to be killed on active service for centuries. The Duke's watch had stopped at thirty-two minutes after take-off. At first it was thought that all the crew had been killed. But one man survived: the gunner in the tail turret of the Sunderland. As the plane had struck the ground, the tail had broken off and Andrew Jack was somehow cushioned from death, though badly burned and injured. When he first recovered he searched for survivors and, finding none, made a slow and painful way across the moor until he came to a small cottage, three hours after the main search party had found the plane.

Then followed an enquiry into what had happened in these thirty-two minutes and how the highly-experienced Sunderland crew, reinforced by their Commanding Officer, a navigational expert, could have made the kind of mistake that even the rawest beginner was trained to avoid—beware of high ground. There must have been an explanation why the pilot and navigating crew, knowing their course, kept descending over ground which they knew from maps contained peaks. There had to be some explanation, but the Court of Enquiry failed to find it. The Court's findings were that the accident occurred because the aircraft was flown on a track other than that indicated in the flight plan given to the pilot, and at too low an altitude to clear the rising ground on the track. While this was evident, there was no explanation as to how such a tragic error could have occurred. The Court expressed the opinion that the responsibility for the mistake in airmanship lay with the Captain, the usual let-out when the Captain invariably gets the blame, even though the error was committed by one of his crew. An investigation indicated that the aircraft was in good shape and there were no engine or structural failures. The only thing that is certain is that something went wrong, or something occurred to confuse or mislead the crew. The truth will never be known and the incident, involving an eminent member of the Royal Family in wartime, is now yet one of the many mysteries of the air, this time with a rather interesting Highland association.

Mysteries still occur in the Highlands, involving all the elements which go to make them a talking point for future generations. Some will inevitably increase in 'folk' stature until they assume a place which may be out of all proportion to their actual import- ance. However, be that as it may, when mysteries do occur in our times they present all the same trappings which mysterious happen- ings must have offered in times past: shadowy witnesses, uncertain evidence, opinions and series of inconclusions. One such mystery reached the headlines of the Scottish Press at the end of 1975 with the strange case of 'the pilot who never came back'.

The bizarre death of ex-fighter pilot Peter Gibbs will probably remain an unsolved mystery. Gibbs was an outstanding child violinist who made his first radio broadcast at the age of eight. He learned to fly Spitfires at the age of twenty and in 1941 flew in European operations as a fighter pilot. Completely fearless, he was shot down seven times, in each instance to parachute to safety: experiences which left little impression on him. After the war, he joined different orchestras and, in 1948, became a member of a highly-acclaimed string quartet before linking up with the London Symphony Orchestra. Later he joined the BBC Scottish Orchestra, became its leader in 1964. After a varied career he became leader for a season at the Royal Opera House, London. He was finally a business man, builder and property owner with plans for buying a hotel in the Western Isles or on the west of Scotland. On Christmas Eve in 1975, Peter Gibbs took off from the Glenforsa air-strip on the Isle of Mull in a single-engined Cessna aircraft—and disappeared, just before his fifty-fifth birthday.

Gibb's plane rose off from the airstrip runway at night, about 21.25 hours, with the help of a friend who provided two torch-lights at the end of the runway perimeters. Ordinarily this was a foolhardy action. But it was even more so, because Gibbs was flying illegally. His pilot's licence had expired a year before and he had been told by the Department of Trade that he would be ex-pected to undergo a general flying test before it could be renewed. In vain, Gibb's friend waited for the return of the plane. When it failed to appear, the police were informed, and a search mounted. But no trace was found of either plane or the pilot.

Gibb's body was eventually found about four months after-wards. A medical examination indicated that he died from ex-posure. There was no sign of the plane. The body was found by a Mull shepherd less than a mile from the Glenforsa airstrip, beside a fallen tree and not far from two freshwater lochs. A number of theories were put forward at the Sheriff Court at Oban which looked into the possible causes of the fatal accident, on which a jury returned a formal verdict.

Firstly, it was thought that the plane's engines had stalled in mid-air and that Gibbs, in the darkness, had made a soft landing in a freshwater loch. Somehow he had managed to extricate him-self and, possibly in a state of shock, had wandered in the dark on the moor, before finally succumbing to the cold, and dying beside the fallen tree. Another theory was that Gibbs had jumped from the plane before it carried on in the air over a sea-shelf on the near-by shore. But the objection to this theory was that the body carried no injury consistent with jumping from a plane, even at low level, unless freak conditions prevailed. As there was found no salt-water traces on the body it was not thought he had survived a sea crash, to manage to make safety on the shore. A third theory was that the plane had gone in the opposite direction, away from seawards, to plunge into a forest; but this would have carried Gibbs with it. Aerial surveys by the RAF over the island of Mull have revealed no trace of a crashed plane.

As this chapter is being proofed and the book nearing its completion, nine months' of intensive searching have revealed absolutely no trace of an Inverness mother and her three-year-old child. Their car was found burning in a layby on the southward road from Inverness to Perth. Investigation revealed that no one was burned to death in the vehicle. The two missing persons have completely vanished with the police faced with diminishing and slender clues— yet another mystery to be added to the Highland catalogue.

SEVEN

Latter-day Affairs

The period after the Battle of Culloden is often hailed as one in which law and order were imposed, albeit fitfully, on the Highland region. However, the arm of the law was ever short and this circumstance allowed for crimes against persons to be committed by those who knew with reasonable certainty that they would get away with their misdeeds. Thus, it should come as no surprise that the Highlands, in common with other parts of Scotland and the British Isles generally, provided not a few instances of criminal assaults leading to murder and homicide. Generally, however, when the law and its facilities became stronger and gained more respect, the people of the Highlands could pride themselves on being among the most law-abiding citizens in Britain. Particularly in the remote parts, the sight of a policeman was rare because perhaps, the communities themselves, being close-knit, tended to exercise sufficient restraints to deter serious crimes against innocent persons. Violence, however, has always lurked just beneath the skin of any society and the Highlands have contributed their share of incidents. In modern times the increase in the number of violent deaths has been more than disturbing in a Scottish context. From thirty-eight murders in Scotland in 1974 the figure increased to sixty violent deaths in the first six months of 1976. The statistic which causes the most concern is the number of young boys now being convicted of murder, with the age of murderers moving down in recent years. Many of these sad cases are linked with under-age drinking, resulting in, as one Scottish Judge said in 1976: "meaningless and motiveless" murders.

Over the past two centuries there have been a number of interesting cases involving murder. However, on a statistical basis, the low incidence of killings in the Highland region perhaps indicates that the folk were generally law-abiding—even when seen against the background of violence which Highland history has shown was once a fact of life, of living and of death.

In the month of September, 1812, at the Circuit Court of Inverness, Robert Ferguson was tried for the murder of Captain Charles Munro, of the 42nd Regiment, at a smithy in the Parish of Resolis, Ross-shire. Captain Munro had entered the smithy at five o'clock in the afternoon on 2nd June in that year. Ferguson entered shortly afterwards and began to swear at the captain, who retaliated by pushing him outside. Ferguson returned later with an open knife and plunged the weapon into the captain's side. He died the following evening. He remarked before he died that "he wished he had fallen on the field of battle". Ferguson was convicted of murder and executed at Inverness in the following November. A newspaper report noted: "Great concourse of spectators. Prisoner addressed the multitude in Gaelic, acknowledging the justice of his sentence. He then made many similar reflections on his own situation, and stated that till some time after he was confined to the prison in Inverness, he had not had access to the Scriptures; that by the benevolence of well-disposed persons in Inverness, he was soon taught to read and that ever since the Word of God had been his only comfort."

Six years later, in 1818, two men from Rothiemurchus were tried on a charge of having murdered Alexander Robertson, late Ensign Royal Westminster Middlesex Regiment. It appears that all three were at a party and then retired to a boathouse at Rothiemurchus to continue drinking. They took a great deal of whisky toddy and indulged in a lot of horseplay, which concluded in a series of scuffles in which Robertson received a blow on the temple that caused him to reel, and "inflicted a wound from which blood proceeded". At the trial, the question was put: Was Robertson killed by a blow or by natural causes some five weeks afterwards? In the event, one man was convicted and sentenced to fourteen years transportation on a charge of culpable homicide while the second man was acquitted.

In February 1830 two crimes were reported by the *Inverness*

Courier. The first concerned the murder of a lonely woman, Helen MacKenzie, aged sixty, in her cottage near Achnagarron, Easter Ross. The motive in this crime was robbery, because it was believed locally that she possessed a store of money. The murderer was never found. The second crime was one involving the robbery of a pedlar near Grantown. He was attacked and left insensible by the roadside. The poor man was robbed of £23 and goods valued at £30. Again the perpetrators were never found. Pedlars and similar itinerants were popular victims of attack-and-run assaults. In the following year, Murdoch Grant, was murdered at Assynt by Hugh MacLeod, after the pedlar's money and goods. Later in 1830 there were four murder cases at the Inverness Autumn Circuit. In one case the culprit was pronounced insane. In the second case, the crime was not proven. The third trial produced a verdict of not guilty while the fourth was the trial of the above-mentioned Hugh MacLeod.

Three years later, in 1833: "At the Inverness Circuit Court numerous charges of assault were heard. The Presiding Judge said there were more cases of assault tried at this circuit than in all parts of Scotland united. 'The people of the Highlands,' he said, 'seemed in this respect to be a people living without the law'." The editor of the local newspaper thought this statement to be a little exaggerated, but he expressed the hope that influential persons would "exert increased activity to try to repress an offence which has become a reproach and disgrace to us, and which seems, unfortunately, to be on the increase".

An interesting highlight of the time was raised in 1833, when Inverness Town Council was reported as being of the opinion that the services of Donald Ross, the hangman, might be dispensed with. He had been appointed as executioner in 1812, with a salary of £16 *per annum*, with many other perks of the trade. He was allowed fifty-six peats weekly from the tacksman of the Petty Customs in Inverness; a bushel of coals out of every cargo of English coals imported into the town; a piece of coal, as large as he could carry, out of every cargo of Scotch coals imported; a fish from every creel or basket of fish brought to the market. By 1833 Ross had attended only three executions at an overall cost of £400 per item. The previous hangman of Inverness had experienced an untimely end. He had had occasion to go to Elgin on professional business and was "attacked on his return, about Forres, by a mob of mischievous boys and lads, who maltreated him in such a shameful manner that he died on the spot. The most active of the mob were, however, tried and transported".

On 5th May 1834, William Noble was tried for the murder of William Ritchie at the Circuit Court of Inverness. He was convicted and sentenced to be hanged at Elgin. Aged only twenty, he was executed on 31st May 1834. As there had been no execution at Elgin for seventy years, and the city had no resident executioner, a hangman was procured from Dundee at the charge of £12, exclusive of travelling expenses. "This plan," said a local newspaper, "of engaging executioners only when required and not for life according to current use and wont, will soon become general. It will be a saving to the Burghs and two to three hangmen will do for all Scotland."

In April 1835 the body of a middle-aged woman was found in a ruined hut in a tree plantation on the low heights of Kilcoy, in the Black Isle. Although it had been carefully covered up with turf and stones, the ravages of weather and wind had exposed a glove, part of a veil, and a shoe. These objects were noticed by some people in a party of women and children at work in the plantation. The authorities were immediately alerted and the news of the gruesome discovery went around the countryside like wildfire and speculation was the order of the day. However, it did not take the authorities too long to obtain identification of the body, which eventually led to the arrest of John Adam. The body was that of Jane Brechin, a native of Montrose. John Adam, from the same town on the east coast of Scotland, was, at the time of his arrest, living in two places: at Dingwall and in Inverness, and living under the assumed name of John Anderson. Adam had known Jane Brechin when he was younger and indeed, the affair had reached the stage where marriage was being considered. However, Adam left Montrose to enter the Army and it was while stationed in England that he befriended a girl, named Elliot, whom he later married. The couple then moved to live in Dingwall, where he worked as a labourer. Perhaps the marriage ties proved too oppressive; or perhaps it was simply lack of sufficient cash which led Adam to return to Montrose where he renewed his acquaintance with Jane Brechin. The latter, still susceptible to Adam's charms, was persuaded to sell up the stock in her small shop and draw from the bank some £113. The couple then 'eloped' from Montrose to Inverness, where they took lodgings in Chapel Street, which still stands today in the town. But the problem of having a wife living some twenty miles farther north in Dingwall worried Adam, and he frequently left his 'wife' in Inverness to visit his legitimate partner. Eventually the double life became difficult to cope with and Adam resolved to finalize the matter. He invited Jane Brechin to go with him to visit friends on the Black Isle. Both murderer and the unsuspecting victim crossed the small ferry at Kessock and made their way to Mulbuie where he set upon his partner and killed her, burying her body where it was eventually discovered. After his arrest, Adam denied that he had done the deed. But the jury at his trial found him guilty and the judge pronounced sentence of death. A newspaper report of the time said: "He slept soundly the night before his death, and in his waking hours talked with his warders about his adventures in the Army and other indifferent topics."

The execution took place at the Longman, Inverness. Owing to the density of the crowd which had gathered to watch, the culprit was taken to the gallows in a cart. He was dressed in a long black coat, provided for the occasion. The spectators numbered over 8,000. Adam, to the end, refused to confess his crime. Afterwards, however, it turned out that he had acknowledged it to a fellow prisoner, to be made known after his death. His execution was the last to take place at Inverness.

What is recorded as the last duel fought in Scotland took place in the spring of 1844 in a field on the outskirts of Stornoway, Lewis, thus giving the town a rather unusual claim to fame in keeping with the warlike element which the Western Isles have contributed to the history of Scotland, though often that was in retaliation for royal and political interference in Hebridean affairs.

The combatants were Mr Macleay, Collector of Customs, Stornoway, and Mr Lewis MacIver, Tacksman of Gress Farm, about six miles north of the town. The latter owned extensive properties in the town and was, in addition, a fishcurer, general merchant and shipowner. The duel was the result of a quarrel between the two men in which the collector accused MacIver of carrying on an extensive system of smuggling. There was in fact at this time a great deal of illegal trafficking in the Highlands. Distilling was carried on with particular intensity on many farms in Lewis and there was what was known as 'the trade' to and from the Faroe Islands, where spirits of all kinds could be purchased from the Danes at a cheap price and imported secretly into Lewis and ports on the north-west mainland coast such as Lochinver. The accusation by the collector was taken as a great insult, though it contained more than a grain of truth. However, the fair face of honour must always be defended and MacIver, who was "very fiery", resented the impeachment. The accusation having been made publicly, MacIver had no option but to challenge the collector to a duel. The latter, equally impetuous, accepted and no time was lost in agreeing to a time and a place for the duel, and that pistols should be the weapons.

Wasting no time, they contacted a master tailor of the name of MacKenzie who was tenant of a field outside Stornoway, and he agreed that the duel could take place there. The trio then made their way to the field and as soon as they arrived the combatants stripped to their shirts and told MacKenzie to act as umpire. There were no seconds, MacKenzie being the only other person in the field and witness to the event at close quarters. The duellists fired simultaneously, but owing possibly to the excited state of both men, they both missed. Apparently, MacKenzie was satisfied with the result of his first shot and did not ask that a second round should be fired. As for the collector, still taken aback at the rapidity of events, agreed that the matter should end there and then. Both men shook hands, dressed, and returned to the town. MacKenzie went even so far as to invite the collector into his house for refreshment.

But that was not quite the end of the business. While the duel was in progress, several persons passing the field witnessed the event and the news was sent round the town like wildfire. Eventually it got to the ears of Mr Donald Munro, a solicitor who was also Procurator Fiscal for the island. Dependent on crime cases for his fees, which had been dwindling of late, Munro saw an opportunity for a betterment of his financial situation. Immediately investigating the matter, he precognosed several witnesses, including MacKenzie the tailor. The case papers were duly sent to the Crown Counsel in Edinburgh but, to Munro's surprise and chagrin, the papers were returned with instructions to take no further proceedings. If nothing else, the case gave the island a talking point for weeks afterwards.

A son of MacIver's, John MacIver, was a Bank Agent at Dingwall; he was involved in what became known as the Mountgerald Poison Case, which created a great sensation at the time.

MacIver had given a dinner at his house, at which a party of gentlemen were guests, among whom were two Roman Catholic priests and a local proprietor named MacKenzie of Mountgerald, Ross-shire. These three died of poisoning caused by Monkshood root being taken from the garden of MacIver's house in mistake for horse-radish. A public investigation was held by the local Fiscal and Sir Douglas MacLagan was sent from Edinburgh to Dingwall in connection with the post-mortem examination of the three bodies. As the cook had some of the vegetable still in her possession, the cause of the tragedy was soon discovered. Lord Lovat, a Roman Catholic, drove over furiously on hearing of the death of the priests in a Protestant house, in order to see that a proper investigation was made. But, on learning that the mistress of the house and the cook were also Catholics, his suspicions were appeased and the circumstances of the deaths were shown to be quite accidental. Another of the guests, a well-known cattle dealer in his day, was John MacDonald of London, who saved his life by walking about outside until he had worked off the effects of the poison which had killed his companions at the fateful dinner.

During the last century the fishing population of the Highlands and Island of Scotland 'followed the herring', as the great shoals of fish swam predictably round the shores of the British Isles. By the end of the last century there was no fishing port between

Lowestoft and Lerwick in the Shetland Islands where the Gaelic of the Outer Hebrides could not be heard during the summer months, from fishermen as well as the fisher girls who followed in the wake of their menfolk in great numbers. The flourishing town of Wick in Caithness was a popular port, presenting a thrilling sight with its harbour crammed with hundreds of wherries and other fishing craft with masts towering into the sky like a rope-tangled denuded forest of bare trees. However, there was no love lost between the Wickers and the Hebrideans, and every opportunity was taken by the former to bait the incomers. This attitude led to the famous riots which broke out on the night of Saturday 27th August 1859 and which lasted a whole week, known in Hebridean tradition as 'Sabaid Mhor Wick'.

Traditionally it is reported that an apple caused the initial disturbance. In Lewis it is said that a young man from the village of Balallan saw a Wick youth of about his own age try to take an apple from a small boy and he took the latter's part. The older Wick youth resented the intrusion of an incomer and a fight ensued. In no time at all the fight had attracted a crowd of spectators, including two local police officers who immediately apprehended the Lewis lad but left the Wick youth alone. They took their prisoner to the Court House, in spite of several attempts by Highland fishermen to release him, attempts which were frustrated by local Wick men rallying round the constables. A fisherman from Lewis, the young lad's father, a man noted for both strength and courage, went to his ship and, with the aid of his crew, unshipped the mast and, with the further aid of many willing assistants, marched up to the door of the Court House with the intention of using it as a battering ram. But this attempt to breach more than the peace failed.

Soon scuffles were taking place all over the town. Stones were thrown at the Court House and things looked decidedly ugly, a situation which alarmed the magistrates of the town. Police batons were issued to all of the local men who were willing to take them. Old muskets and pistols were unearthed which had not seen the light of day for generations. The Highlanders were unarmed, but were at no great loss in their own defence; paving stones were ripped up and barrel staves used as weapons. The Highlanders, however, were finally driven away in a disorderly mob from the neighbourhood of the Court House and across the Wick River where they reorganized themselves for another attack. The townspeople by this time were thoroughly alarmed. Many of them stayed indoors for the rest of the week. Every shop was shut and strongly shuttered; doors were securely locked and barred. The sound of rioting could be heard all over the place, both day and night.

That fateful Sabbath passed with no person knowing what the following day would bring, because the weather was brewing up for a storm and the Highland boats, which would normally have left the port for the fishing were still tied up in the harbour. So it turned out. None of the boats could go to sea and the idle fishermen roamed through Wick; trouble flared up again and again and carried on throughout the week. The locals used the occasion to settle old scores on their neighbours, the Highlanders being blamed for the disturbances. The young Lewis lad's father, strong though he was, was attacked a number of times. Twice he was thrown by a mob into the sea, but in each case he took one of his opponents with him, for the pleasure of the company. Sailors, fully armed, were landed from the revenue cutter *Princess Royal*, which happened to be in the vicinity; but as they were insufficient to quell the disorders, H.M.S. *Jackal* was ordered north from Berwick and her men patrolled the streets of Wick to keep the peace.

To secure that peace, the civil authorities sent for the help of the military in Edinburgh and a detachment of the West York Rifles was hurriedly dispatched north. However, the efforts of a few people, including the minister of the Free Church in Tongue, Sutherland, a Gaelic speaker, brought the disturbed town to some order. But the memory of the injustice of the original affair stuck in the minds of the Highlanders for years afterwards, and it was to be a long time indeed before Wickers and Highlanders became reconciled to each other once more.

The 17th February 1899 saw the Abernethy murder trial. In the previous December, at Milton of Tulloch, in the Parish of Abernethy, Inverness-shire, Allan MacCallum was made prisoner and lodged in the prison at Inverness. He was charged with the murder of Thomas King, a police constable, having discharged a loaded gun at him and killed him. He was tried at Inverness Castle, where a plea of insanity was lodged on the grounds that he was for many years in South America where his stay there was considered sufficiently long to have dislodged his mind under the Patagonian sun. In fact, MacCallum had been considered insane six years previously in 1892. He got fifteen years penal servitude. The case created much interest all over Scotland. A local newspaper reported: "Extra work was thrown upon the telegraph staff of the Post Office when 45,000 words were telegraphed to all parts of Scotland. Six sets of Wheatstone automatic apparatus were kept running at a high rate of speed from 10.30 a.m. to 23.30 p.m. . . . . The wires were cleared exactly in ten minutes after the last batch of copy had been handed in." Thirty journalists were in the court to hear that MacCallum had previously been fined for some rather trivial offence but did not pay it. When he saw the police outside his house, he thought they were there to arrest him for the non-payments of the fine and jumped to the wrong conclusions, taking fear, with such tragic results.

On 14th December 1900:

The man Stewart, whose skull was fractured by two tinker brothers, also named Stewart, was in a precarious condition in Dingwall. Their capture was the result of a long chase by police constables who scoured Ross-shire for a week. The mother of the two accused was watched. Police became suspicious of her movements, as she travelled in her cart during the night, and hid in secluded places during the day. She travelled very fast, and had to change horses at Alness, from whence the police kept on her track till she reached Strathcarron, where she pitched camp in a dense wood. A constable lay on the ground a whole night watching her camp and at last his vigilance was rewarded by seeing one of the two accused creeping through the bushes and enter the tent. The constable followed and had his man in handcuffs before he had a chance of resistance. The prisoner was in a terrible state, soaked to the skin, gaunt, and starving as he had travelled over the mountains from Ardgay to Strathcarron, for six days, in terrible weather. Another constable relieved his comrade and in watching the camp and after some time was able to capture the other brother in his mother's tent.

M

The month of October, 1902, saw the Cromarty murder trial, which referred to the murder, in July 1901, of James Junor by assault and kicking. The murderer was Alexander Mowatt, a farm servant at Udale, near Cromarty. The deed was done through an excess of drinking, according to a deposition taken when Junor was near the point of death. Mowatt was found guilty of culpable homicide but there was a recommendation to mercy and he was sent to prison for twelve months. Another incident which was caused through drink was when a farm labourer from Croy in Inverness-shire died of wounds in 1903. He was killed by his cousin, who received a sentence of eighteen months' imprisonment.

On the 22nd October 1934, the dead body of a scantily-clothed woman was found lying in a park on the outskirts of Inverness and created something of a sensation in the town. The discovery was made by a drover who, entering the field to collect some cattle, noticed one of the animals beside what he thought was a bundle. On investigation he was horrified to see the body and made all haste into Inverness to inform the police. Later, after some intensive enquiries, the police charged a vagrant aged twenty-two years with the crime. John MacPhee was charged: ". . . that he did beat her with his fists and killed her with his booted feet on the face, head and body, and did murder her". The accused at the time of the crime was drunk with methylated spirits which he had been drinking in the company of both the dead woman and her mother. The jury took only forty minutes to decide that he was guilty of culpable homicide and MacPhee was sentenced to eight years' penal servitude. In the same year another case of serious assault was heard in Inverness at which a man was accused of housebreaking and assaulting a crofter of eighty-five years of age by "beating him with a stick to the effusion of blood and the danger of his life". The old man could speak very little English and an interpreter had to be brought into court to interpret his evidence which was given in Gaelic. The charge was acquitted.

In 1938 a man from the island of Lewis was convicted of the crime of murdering his wife and was sentenced to death at the Circuit Court in Inverness. He was afterwards certified to be insane and ordered to be kept in custody. The case, which was the first of its kind in Lewis for decades, was one of jealousy, growing out of a religious mania. At the same Circuit trials, presided over by Lord Cockburn, there were several cases of violent personal assault which "we are told is the most common crime in the Highlands".

Some thirty years later, in 1969, the island of Lewis rocked with horror at the news of a brutal killing of an old woman in the village of Brue, on the west coast of the island. The body was found by a neighbour who had noticed that the curtains had not been drawn aside in the usual manner. He went into the house, through the scullery door which, in common with doors in the island even today, are seldom locked, indicating the respect for persons and their property in such communities. He called out but got no reply. He went further into the house and found, in a bedroom the old lady lying on the floor in a pool of blood; she had received serious head injuries. A clock was found on the bedroom floor with its glass broken and stopped at 5.55. The police and detectives were immediately called in for investigation and eventually a George MacLeod appeared in Inverness to plead not guilty to the charge of "striking her repeatedly on the head with an unknown instrument, stealing from her a sum of money and a handkerchief, and murdering her". Over eighty witnesses were cited to appear from the Crown, while the defence was content with six witnesses.

At the trial, held in Inverness, evidence was given that the deceased Miss Mary MacKenzie, was somewhat eccentric, and had old newspapers lying about the house, and also had sums of money wrapped up in pieces of newspaper. The trial excited great public interest for it was one of the extremely rare cases of murder on the island of Lewis in more than a century. Long queues lined up outside the High Court of Justiciary in Inverness before the morning and afternoon sessions.

The trial proved to be long and complicated. The evidence led for the prosecution was circumstantial, but it was obvious that the motive for the murder was robbery. The Advocate Deputy submitted that both the murder and the robbery were committed by the same person. He maintained that the circumstances of the murder and theft pointed to there having been committed by a person with local knowledge—someone who knew that there was money in the house and who knew where to look for it. In particular, the finding of seven consecutively-numbered banknotes issued by the British Linen Bank in the accused's suitcase was of major significance, since old-age pensioners were always paid in these notes, whereas the accused was paid for his weaving work in notes of the Bank of Scotland and the Bank of England, and it was inconceivable that he could have got seven consecutively-numbered Linen Bank notes in change from a travelling shop where he had made some purchases. The Advocate Deputy also reminded the jury in his summing up that the accused had been paid £47 19s. which he was due by the National Insurance office in Stornoway on 15th November, mostly in Linen Bank notes and described as a "sudden acquisition of wealth".

In the defence of the accused, it was pointed out that he had no record of violence and possibly the wrong man had been charged. The problem was a matter of the deductions to be made from the evidence presented to the Court: "these deductions made a chain strung out by fibres of the imagination which could be blown away by a breath of air". There was nothing to connect George MacLeod with the murder house or with the murder.

The Lord Justice Clerk, Lord Grant, in his address to the jury which lasted one and a half hours, also said that the case for the Crown was wholly dependent on circumstantial evidence. The jury took one hour and twenty minutes to return a unanimous verdict of 'not proven', thus leaving the accused free and the whole case to be left in a state of suspended animation to be speculated on until the matter is perhaps resolved at some distant date in the future.

Selected Bibliography

Glen-Albyn; Tales and Truths of the Central Highlands (Fort Augustus, 1906)

Home Life of the Highlanders, 1400–1746 (Glasgow, 1911)

Life of Hugh MacLeod, Assynt (Inverness, 1889, 3rd ed.)

Anderson, P., *Culloden Moor* (Stirling, 1930)

Bain, G., *The Lordship of Petty* (Nairn, 1925)

Bardens, D., *Ghosts and Hauntings* (London, 1965)

Barnett, R., *The Road to Rannoch and the Summer Isles* (Edinburgh, 1924)

Blaikie, W. B., *Origins of the Forty-five* (Edinburgh, 1916)

Burt, E., *Letters from a Gentleman in the North of Scotland* (London, 1822, 5th ed.)

Campbell, J. F., *Popular Tales of the West Highlands* (Edinburgh, 1862)

Celtic Magazine (Inverness, 1875–1888)

Coxe-Hippisley, A. D., *Haunted Britain* (London, 1973)

Chambers, R., *Domestic Annals of Scotland* (Edinburgh, 1885)

Dougal, J. W., *Island Memories* (Edinburgh, 1937)

Drever, H., *Tales of the Scottish Clans* (Edinburgh, 1931)

Duff, A., *Scotland's War Losses* (Glasgow, 1946)

Forbes, R., *The Lyon in Mourning* (Edinburgh, 1895; Edinburgh, 1975)

Gaelic Society of Inverness: *Transactions* (Inverness, in progress)

Gregory, D., *History of the Western Highlands of Scotland* (reprint, Edinburgh, 1975)

Grimble, I., *The Chief of MacKay* (London, 1965)

Inverness Field Club, *The Hub of the Highlands* (Edinburgh, 1975)

Johnston, T., *The History of the Working Classes in Scotland* (reprint, Wakefield, 1974)

Kilgour, W. T., *Lochaber in War and Peace* (Stirling, 1908)

MacArthur, W., *The Appin Murder and the Trial of James Stewart* (London, 1960)

MacDonald, D., *Tales and Traditions of the Lews* (Stornoway, 1967)

MacGregor, A., *Feuds of the Clans* (Stirling, 1907)

MacKay, W., *Highland Weapons* (Inverness, 1970)

MacKenzie, A., *The History of the Highland Clearances* (Inverness, 1883)

MacKenzie, O., *A Hundred Years in the Highlands* (reprint, London, 1949)

MacKenzie, W. C., *The Book of the Lews* (Paisley, 1919)

——, *The Highlands and Isles of Scotland* (Edinburgh, 1937)

——, *A Short History of the Scottish Highlands and Isles* (Stirling, 1906)

MacKerral, A., *Kintyre in the Seventeenth Century* (Edinburgh, 1948)

MacLeay, K., *Historical Memoirs of Rob Roy and Clan Macgregor* (including original notices of Lady Grange) (Edinburgh, 1881)

MacLeod, R. C., *The MacLeods* (Edinburgh, 1928)

Matheson, A., *The Appin Murder* (Inverness, 1975)

Old Statistical Account for Scotland (Edinburgh, 1792)

Pennant, T., *A Tour in Scotland in 1769; A Tour in Scotland and Voyage to the Hebrides* (London, 1772)

Prebble, J., *The Highland Clearances* (London, 1963)

——, *Glencoe* (London, 1964)

——, *Culloden* (London, 1967)

Scott, Sir W., *The Highland Clans, With a Particular Account of Rob Roy and the Macgregors* (Edinburgh, 1856)

Scottish History Society, *Proceedings and Publications* (in progress)

Scottish Studies: "Massacre of Dunaverty", Vol. 19, 1975

Swire, O., *Skye, the Island and its Legends* (Glasgow, 1961)

——, *The Highlands and their Legends* (Edinburgh, 1963)

——, *The Inner Hebrides and their Legends* (Glasgow, 1964)

——, *The Outer Hebrides and their Legends* (Edinburgh, 1966)

Thompson, F., *The Ghosts, Spirits and Spectres of Scotland* (Aberdeen, 1972)

Wordsworth, D., *Journals, 1798–1828* (London, 1924)

Youngson, A. J., *Beyond the Highland Line* (London, 1974)

Index